Nine Yards of Silk and Three Pieces of Jade

By
Sue Exton

Grosvenor House
Publishing Limited

All rights reserved
Copyright © Sue Exton, 2025

The right of Sue Exton to be identified as the author of this
work has been asserted in accordance with Section 78
of the Copyright, Designs and Patents Act 1988

The book cover is copyright to Sue Exton

This book is published by
Grosvenor House Publishing Ltd
Link House
140 The Broadway, Tolworth, Surrey, KT6 7HT.
www.grosvenorhousepublishing.co.uk

This book is sold subject to the conditions that it shall not, by way of
trade or otherwise, be lent, resold, hired out or otherwise circulated
without the author's or publisher's prior consent in any form of
binding or cover other than that in which it is published and
without a similar condition including this condition being
imposed on the subsequent purchaser.

This book is a work of fiction. Any resemblance to
people or events, past or present, is purely coincidental.

A CIP record for this book
is available from the British Library

Paperback ISBN 978-1-83615-167-8
Hardback ISBN 978-1-83615-168-5
eBook ISBN 978-1-83615-169-2

This book – the second in a series – tells the story of a family who have lived with the horrors life throws at them. This book contains sex and violence and tells of a young girl's struggles to overcome repeated nightmares with the support of her grandmother, who is always there for her.

With a lifetime of secrets herself, the older woman finds herself reliving her own unspeakable past just to help her granddaughter survive.

This is the second in a series. The first is entitled, *Damaged Mind* by Doctor Valerie.

THIS IS AN ADULT BOOK CONTAINING SEX AND VIOLENCE.

This is the story of a young girl called Aveling, just trying to find her place in life and fighting for her own identity. Now just turned sixteen, Aveling leaves her grandmother's Chinese home to rejoin her English father in London, only to be sent on her way by his new wife, who is just a few years older than herself.

Enrolled at a private boarding school, she meets another girl with no restraints, and Aveling's life becomes one long nightmare. As she lays her head down to sleep, how can she shake off those feelings of dread so she can move on with her life? Just when she starts to feel safe, her nightmares start all over again. When will they ever end?

PROLOGUE

I left my home in China, hoping for a new life with my father back in his own country of England. But when I arrived, I was sent on my way by his new wife, into a world where I had no idea of what was about to happen. I was so naïve. How could I have been so stupid to believe in and trust so many bad people. Yet I never thought for one moment that I would end up wanting to kill them.

*

Aveling felt the damp rising into her back from the wet ground. She tried to open her eyes, only to close them again, as the rain fell heavier and heavier on her face and she wondered, *Am I still alive?*

As she tried to move, she felt no movement in her limbs and her voice deserted her. She thought she must be dead, but then she felt a pain she had never felt before. She tried to move, but something was pushing her harder and harder, firmly keeping her from moving, and the wet ground beneath her felt colder and colder. It felt like her body no longer belonged to her, then just for a few seconds she managed to open her eyes.

A face was just a few inches above hers. And while the bright blue eyes and blond curly hair left her with a sense of an angel's presence, those same eyes turned her cold and all she felt was fear. At that moment, she believed she was indeed dead.

CHAPTER 1: FIRST MOVE

"I don't want to go, Dad. Please, please, Dad, I want to stay with you."

"Sorry, Aveling, but I promised your grandmother that you could stay with her until I get things sorted out in the UK. She is really looking forward to you visiting, and it could be an exceedingly long time before you will get the chance to see her again. Once we leave China, and return to England, it will be some time before I get my next assignment. So, just be a good girl and pack your things up.

"Don't worry, Aveling, it is just while I get everything set up in London, but you know the government could send me anywhere. I did think about letting you stay with your mother in Paris, but as you know she is now living with that useless man who claims to be a male model, and God knows how he would treat you.

"At least this way, I know your grandmother will keep you safe. Now, no more of your nonsense, go and pack your things. Don't bother with any larger items, as I will ship them over to London with the rest of my things at the end of the month. It will take me a little time to find you a new school, so just have some patience, and I will get you to join me in London as quickly as I can."

To Aveling, it seemed like her whole word was falling apart. It didn't matter how much pleading she did, she was going to be left alone in China, with her old grandmother who lived in the middle of nowhere. Since the end of the freehold of Hong Kong, and its return into China's hands, she had known that her diplomat father would be reassigned. But to be so far apart just seemed unbearably cruel.

Aveling did speak Chinese, as her mother had been born there and worked for a time as a translator in the British Embassy, which is where she met Aveling's father. But her mother had left to move in with her lover in Paris just a few years before, and Aveling had never got on too well with her Chinese grandmother, and her grandfather had passed away several years before. It was such a contrast from living in the modern Embassy, where she had access to the internet and all modern technology, to her grandmother's house in the country, which was like a step back in time by about forty years.

The difference in cultures was huge. At the Embassy, she was allowed to dress in modern clothes, but as soon as she arrived at her grandmother's, she knew her dresses would all have to be longer, makeup was not allowed, and she would be treated like a six-year-old. There was no internet, no mod cons, and the old woman told the same old stories over and over again, which drove Aveling crazy.

It was a chilly day when she arrived. Although she loved her grandmother, they had little in common. But she knew that all the staff would make a big fuss of her. They were always desperate to find out all about what was happening in Hong Kong, and new fashions, modern TV, and the internet, were always big topics of conversation. Aveling didn't mind talking with the staff about life in Hong Kong, although she was convinced that some of them didn't believe half of what she told them. However, she was uncomfortable with any questions questioned about things that were happening in the Embassy, as her father had told her from a very young age that she must be discreet.

Usually, once she had answered all the questions she could, she would disappear into one of the outbuildings, feeling more content to be left alone to read a good book. Aveling's mother had always said, "Aveling isn't shy; she is just a little stupid." But the truth was she just didn't have time for her own daughter.

When she married Aveling's dad, the last thing she had wanted was children, but her parents had driven her crazy asking when she was going to make them grandparents. So, after she had Aveling, she lied and told them she could not have any more children.

As Aveling had not seen her grandmother since the previous year, she hoped life with the older woman would be different. With her mother in Paris and father so back in England, Aveling just felt lonely.

Now that she was sixteen and saw herself as a young woman, Aveling thought she would no longer have to comply with all the old rules. But the thing that sent her crazy was the old stories which her grandmother would repeat over and over again. Aveling knew her grandmother loved her, but she would much rather have stayed with her father.

Ever since she heard that the government was recalling her father to London, she had been looking forward to meeting her English side of the family. She knew her English grandmother a little, as she had been over to China for a few visits, but Aveling had never met any other relatives. And any time she asked her father for more family details, all he would do was shrug his shoulders and say, "You'll find out one day for yourself, but don't be too shocked. For now, leave it alone."

Staying with her Chinese grandmother this time seemed so different from normal. Her grandmother was busy packing boxes, and one of the servants explained it was because she was getting ready to move. The old compound she had lived in for most of her life was about to be demolished by the government to build a new road, so her grandmother had no choice but to leave.

The maid revealed that Aveling's grandmother was hoping to move to England, but getting all the paperwork completed would take months. This was, she said, supposed to be a secret from Aveling until everything was sorted. So, she asked Aveling not to let on that she knew anything about it.

As the maid had always been her grandmother's favourite, she was hoping to travel with them to England and had only let on about the plans because she hoped Aveling would be able to help her with her English. Aveling wasn't convinced that the maid would be invited to travel with them, but she felt that was something she needed to keep to herself for now.

This was certainly the first time Aveling had heard anything about her grandmother packing up and getting ready for a move. And while it seemed cruel to move an old woman at that time of her life, Aveling knew that when the Chinese government made up their minds about something, no-one could stop them. If they wanted her grandmother out of her home, she would have no option but to move.

While all the staff were busy packing boxes, Aveling felt a bit lost for something to do. She found her grandmother cleaning out an old cupboard in the back of the bedroom and offered to help.

Suddenly, Aveling pulled out a long silky length of fabric. "Grandmother," she asked, "can I have this? It would make a beautiful scarf."

When her grandmother looked at what Aveling was holding in her hands, she seemed to freeze on the spot. But after a few minutes, she regained her composure.

"Well, Aveling, if my memory serves me right, that was never intended to be a scarf. It's been in our family for such a long time.

Aveling held onto the fabric, stroking it gently, as her grandmother started to explain that many, many years ago a member of her family had been given the long piece of fabric. The old woman had been told that the silk was used to hang a concubine with – nine yards of silk for each one of the concubines. So she presumed that her ancestor must have been one of the royal family's concubines.

"So, the one in my hands, Grandma, has been used to hang a concubine, who was also a member of our family?"

As this was a story Aveling had never heard before, she was all ears, and she sat down on the bed to hear more. Her grandmother went on to explain that the fabric, which was a full nine yards long, 18 inches wide, and made of pure silk, was believed to have been used by her family ancestor called little Gemini. She had been taken as a young girl of just fifteen to become the wife of the ageing emperor. But often, when the emperor died, all the wives and concubines who had not given birth to a child would be hanged together, to travel on to the afterlife with the late emperor. So it was in the concubines' best interest to get pregnant as soon as possible.

If they did not, they would be escorted to a huge, round room, where many lengths of silk – all nine yards long, and one for each concubine – would be hanging from above. When all the women had the silk wrapped around their necks by a palace eunuch, a set of cogs and wheels would begin to turn, and the floor beneath them would drop slowly downwards, leaving them dangling till all the women were strangled to death.

Grandmother had been told that her ancestor had only been married to the old emperor for just six weeks when he died suddenly. Along with the other concubines who had not been pregnant, Gemini was escorted to the hanging room, but didn't understand what was happening to her. She knew nothing about the palace rules, nor had she ever heard anything about the hanging room.

One of the eunuchs was Gemini's blood brother, who plotted to help her escape by fixing the silk in such a way that she would not die. But he needed to quickly explain to Gemini not to move, as she had to make the other eunuchs believe she was dead. When the room was emptied later, the bodies would be escorted out of the city to a cemetery, to be buried with the late emperor. On that occasion, there were fifteen bodies in total. But sometimes an emperor could have hundreds of concubines.

The brother and another eunuch, who was willing to help Gemini, knew that if the new emperor or court ever found out what they'd done, they would face being beheaded along with every member of their families. So everything had to be perfect.

None of them realised that Gemini at that time was just a few weeks pregnant.

Aveling's grandmother explained that the silk scarf now in Aveling's hands was the very same silk that had been around her ancestor's neck on that awful day.

After hanging, the silk of each concubine would be taken down from the rafters and tied around their face, covering the eyes to prevent the woman from seeing her journey into the afterlife. A jade seal – carved from a single piece of jade – would be given to all the girls and women who lived in the palace to allow them to come and go freely around the harem. During the hanging, the jade pass would be tied around the women's waists, to be retrieved afterwards. On that day, it was Gemini's brother who had the job of retrieving them.

At that point in the story, Aveling interrupted. "Grandmother, do you still have the seal?" Her grandmother nodded. "It is in here somewhere."

Aveling was eager to see it and watched anxiously as her grandmother kept digging deeper and deeper into the back of the closet. Eventually, a small velvet bag was pulled clear of the cupboard.

"Found it!" Her grandmother opened the bag, tipped the pouch over the bed, and three pieces fell out.

Aveling pushed the pieces together, making a full circle. With a small hole at the middle to allow a cord to be threaded through, the jade could be carried everywhere by the women from the harem. It allowed others to see instantly that they were the emperor's women. And if a seal was ever lost, the consequences would have been grave.

Aveling's grandmother went on to explain that everyone living in the palace would have needed a pass to go in and out of all the royal compounds in the capital. But while all the concubines had the same seal, the palace's housekeepers carried different and smaller tokens.

Captivated with the story, and hoping her grandmother had more details, Aveling was disappointed when she was told that the older lady had no more information about the nine yards of silk and three pieces of jade.

"Grandma, why have you never told me this story before?"

"It is something we never talk about, because if it was discovered you have royal blood in your veins, there are some people in power who would feel threatened and would stop at nothing to kill you. It's only now that you have turned sixteen and are no longer a child that I can tell you. But," she warned, "to stay safe, you must never repeat what I have told you today."

"Don't worry, Grandma. It's only a story that happened so long ago, so I don't think anybody would take it seriously."

But her grandmother grasped her hand and told her sternly, "No, Aveling, it's not just a story. So promise me you will not tell anyone."

CHAPTER 2: TIME TO FLY

Aveling was finding life difficult at the old farmhouse. Her grandmother had been informed that it could take a year or more until she needed to leave her home, but the staff started to leave one by one. They all knew that the government orders to evacuate could come at any time, so they decided it was better to leave now than wait.

Aveling had a friend called Maylu, who lived down the hill just over a mile away and whose family were not affected by the plans for the new road. Knowing that Aveling would be moving to England at some point, Maylu asked her to come and visit if she ever returned to China. And although Aveling promised she would, she genuinely believed that once she left China she would never see her friend again.

It was almost six months before Aveling finally received a message from her father to confirm that he had made arrangements for her to come to England. Unfortunately, though, her Chinese grandmother was not ready to travel with her at that time. She was still taking care of all the paperwork before she could join the rest of the family in the United Kingdom. In China, paperwork moved very slowly, but Aveling's father explained that there were issues to be resolved with English paperwork, too. It had been decided that on her arrival in England, Aveling's Chinese grandmother would stay for a while with her father's mother, Madam Aveling, at her home, Castle Keys. This would assure the authorities that she would have a good home to live in and someone to support her on arrival.

As she began to pack, Aveling's grandmother asked if she would like to keep the silk and jade, as she had no other grandchildren to give them to. Naturally, Aveling was keen to accept. But when her grandmother handed her the items, she explained in a solemn manner that if Aveling was ever raped, she should keep the family's honour and use the silk for its intended use – death.

Having just turned seventeen a few days before, Aveling was shocked and surprised at her grandmother's comments, but she realised that to the older lady a woman's honour was the most important thing in the world.

As she accepted the gifts, however, she felt her whole body go cold. The hairs raised up on the back of her neck as she held the silk and jade in her hands.

*

On her flight back to England a few days later, Aveling noticed that men were staring at her, which she found very unsettling. When she had lived in the Embassy, the men never paid her any attention because she was the Ambassador's daughter, and the school she attended was an all-girls' school, so this was a new and unnerving experience.

Aveling had been seated in the window seat, next to a young man who never took his eyes off her. Trying to ignore his interest, she looked out of the window and gave all her attention to the landscape below. Once the view of China's landscape disappeared, all she could see was sea. It was going to be a long flight.

A few hours into the flight, they experienced some bad weather. As the plane jolted suddenly, Aveling grabbed the first thing she could and grasped tightly to the arms of her seat. The young man sat beside her sensed her fear and leaned towards her. Gently taking her hand, he explained that it was just a little turbulence which was quite normal, and that she was welcome to squeeze his hand as hard as she liked.

When the air stewardess came round to offer a drink or something to eat, Aveling asked for a glass of lemonade. While she waited, she asked the young man next to her if he could retrieve her shoulder bag from the locker above, and he was only too happy to oblige.

As he chatted away in English, Aveling began to realise that her command of English was not as good as she'd thought, so she politely asked if he could speak a little slower to her.

"Sorry, I didn't realize you were not English," he said, giving her a quizzical look. "My name is Luke. Luke Green."

Aveling had inherited her father's green eyes and jet black hair, and although she was still only five feet two inches tall, her natural beauty shone like a star in the sky. The young man then spoke slowly, asking more questions than she was ready to answer. Giving her name was no problem, but she had no idea of her new address or even a phone number. She did, however, tell him that her father had been an ambassador in the Chinese Embassy but had been recalled to England to await his next posting.

Apparently keen not to lose touch, after they landed the young man gave her his business card with all his details. Slipping the card into her backpack, she headed for the airport exit, pausing briefly to look back over her shoulder. He was heading in the opposite direction but smiled briefly before she lost sight of him.

Although she was convinced she would never see him again, she couldn't help but experience a strange sense of loss.

Outside the airport, she was approached by a stranger holding up her name on a board, who informed her that he had been sent by her father to take her to her new home. Although she wasn't particularly happy about getting into a car with a stranger, she had no idea where her new home was or what it looked like, so felt she had no choice than to climb in.

Everything seemed so strange as she gazed out of the car window, but after more than an hour the driver pulled into a long driveway, then stopped sharply on the gravel stones. As Aveling climbed out of the car, she was greeted by an incredibly attractive young woman, who looked only a few years older than herself, holding a newborn baby.

"Hello, you must be Aveling," the woman smiled. "My name is Carol, and this is your new baby brother Gary."

Aveling's mind went into complete overdrive. How could she have a new baby brother, when it was only about six months since she had last seen her father? He'd never told her he had been seeing anyone.

The shock was clearly evident on Aveling's face. And as they walked into the house, Carol was quick to explain that she had met Aveling's father in Hong Kong, when she worked at the Embassy, then had returned to England with him six months earlier. Suddenly it all made sense why her father hadn't wanted Aveling to travel back with him initially.

But there were more shocks to come.

When her father finally arrived at the house later that evening, the baby was already in bed. Aveling had expected her dad to meet her with a big hug, but the atmosphere around the kitchen table was cold and uncomfortable.

When Carol asked if she could get Aveling anything else to pack for her trip the following day, the young girl turned to her father in surprise. She had only just arrived, and it seemed she was to be shipped off to who knew where!

Seeing her surprise, Carol added, "Oh sorry. I thought your dad had told you. We managed to get you into a private school. You will like it; it's even got a swimming pool."

Looking to her father for confirmation, Aveling was disappointed when his only comment was, "Yes, I am sure you will like it. And

I have arranged a new bank account, so I can send you an allowance in each month."

At that he excused himself and disappeared into his office, which had always been his behaviour if anybody asked him questions he didn't want to answer.

All Aveling could hope for was that she might get him alone the next morning so that they could speak without Carol hovering over him, and before she was to be shipped off to her new school.

However, the next morning when she went downstairs, her father had already left for work. And her packed bags were still in the same place the driver had left them the night before. Aveling had expected to at least be able to sort out her belongings, leaving some of the more bulky items in her new bedroom.

But when she explained that she didn't need to take all the luggage with her, Aveling was informed that she should not leave anything here. Carol explained that she and Aveling's father wouldn't be staying there very long, as he had already been given a new posting to Sweden.

Carol also explained that she had laid out a new school uniform for her to put on, along with a list of instructions.

As Aveling dressed, her mind was spinning. Everything had happened so quickly, and she hadn't even been allowed to visit her English grandmother, who she had been looking forward to seeing. It had been years since they had last met, and Aveling wasn't even sure if her grandmother would recognise her.

When the driver turned up, Aveling expected that Carol would at least be at the door to say goodbye. But she was nowhere to be seen, and instead the driver helped her to load all her luggage into the car.

A few miles up the road, he pulled up at a railway station. When Aveling asked why, the man explained that the school was far too far to drive to, so it had been arranged for her to travel by train. Tickets had been reserved for her to collect at the ticket office.

Left alone on the platform waiting for the train with all her luggage around her, Aveling felt tears welling up. She felt so lost and lonely. She did not know how long the journey would take, or if she could get something to eat.

But as the train pulled in, she shook her head and wiped away the tears, determined not to feel sorry for herself.

Once settled on the train, she took out the list of instructions Carol had given her and studied it more carefully. The first item on the list was how to address the head teacher. and the second was how to send letters via email. Aveling couldn't believe that Carol would think she did not know how to use the internet!

The list was endless, so Aveling rolled it up and stuffed it back inside her backpack. But then she noticed that the list did not include any phone numbers, so if she needed to contact her father or her English grandma quickly, she couldn't.

When she had first arrived, Carol had seemed friendly and helpful, but Aveling couldn't help but think that had been a show to impress her father and the staff. It looked as though Carol was only interested in herself and the new baby.

How on earth did Dad get taken in by such a scheming bitch as Carol? Aveling wondered. She didn't even know if they were married or not. No-one had said anything, but Aveling had noticed a ring on the young woman's finger, and they could have got married when they first arrived in England. *Why didn't Dad tell me anything?* she thought.

Closing her eyes, she tried to pull all the bits of the jigsaw together, as more and more things began to make sense: her father's refusal to take her with him initially; his attitude towards her the previous night; and Carol's desperate rush to get her out of their lives.

Maybe, she thought, *I'm better off without them.*

CHAPTER 3: FITTING IN

Gazing occasionally out of the train window at all the new and unfamiliar sights, Aveling reflected on how much her life had changed in recent years. She clearly remembered the day she had returned from school, at the age of eight or nine, to find that her mother had gone. There was nothing of her mother's left, not even a hairbrush. But when Aveling went to her father's office, she was turned back by his guards, telling her he was too busy.

That evening, she had stayed up late in the hope she would get to see him before bed, but he never came home, and the following morning when she went down for breakfast, he was standing in the kitchen talking to a very smartly dressed woman in a navy blue uniform,

"This is your new nanny," he informed her. "She will be driving you to school and back, and you will do as you are told. Do you understand, girl?"

Aveling must have looked confused, as her father repeated himself, only this time he raised his voice.

Over the following months, her mother was never mentioned. And if Aveling dared to ask a question, she would simply be told to be quiet.

Her nanny, who had arrived from England, clearly did not like Aveling's accent at all. She carried a wooden ruler in her pocket, and if Aveling got words wrong she would feel the ruler over the back of the knuckles – which happened most days.

Many nights, Aveling would cry herself to sleep at night, afraid to make a noise in case the nanny heard from the next room. As the new nanny did not speak a word of Chinese, whenever Aveling wanted something from the kitchen, or something she knew the new nanny would not approve of, she would ask in Chinese. But this only annoyed the woman even more. She was desperate to control Aveling, and had a long list of rules, including only speaking English at home and at school.

Some days Aveling would be caught out speaking in Chinese to some of the staff – something she just did without thinking – so the nanny would discipline her. And if she complained, the punishments would just get harder to bear.

Growing up, Aveling's Chinese mother had arranged for her to attend a school for Chinese children, so she had learned to read and write in the language and only spoke English at home. But when her mother left, and her father changed her school to one that taught only English, Aveling initially struggled. And as she was given more and more homework, the nanny took great satisfaction in whacking her knuckles for even the smallest mistake.

For months, her father told Aveling that her mother had deserted them for another man and blamed her for their split. But it was a year later before she discovered that her mother had left because of her father's affairs.

Every year on her birthday, Aveling would hope to hear from her mother, but she received no card or phone call. It was as if her mother had just fallen off the face of the earth, never to be seen or heard of again.

*

When the train arrived at its final destination, Aveling got off to be met by yet another strange man with a sign. With barely a word spoken, he drove down small country lanes until the space opened to a huge gothic building, like something Aveling had only ever seen in pictures.

As soon as she entered through a huge doorway, she was met by a girl of about the same age. "Hello, you must be Aveling. You will be bunking in with me," the girl announced.

When the girl showed Aveling into a small room with just two beds and not much space for anything else, she realised that everything she had brought from China was not going to fit, so most of her things were left in the cases and just pushed under the bed.

The girl, who introduced herself as Mary, spoke really quickly, making it difficult for Aveling to understand her. But she was left in no doubt when Mary pointed to a huge clock, ticking loudly and hanging on the wall over Aveling's bed, that it was time to go to sleep.

Still baffled by everything that had happened since her arrival in England, Aveling was not ready to sleep, so she lay awake for hours, looking up at the ceiling and wondering how she could sabotage the damn clock.

The next morning, Mary told her she could store any of the extra luggage down in the basement, then took her along what seemed to Aveling to be the world's longest corridor to reach the breakfast room. Just outside the door, Aveling put her hand over her nose and turned to Mary to ask what on earth the smell was.

Mary looked confused. "What smell? All I can smell is breakfast – bacon and sausages – and they smell delicious to me."

In China, Aveling had only eaten white meat and shellfish, so the smell was making her feel a little nauseous. But she tried to concentrate on understanding what Mary was saying as they went into the breakfast room.

After a few minutes, she was still struggling and had to ask Mary to speak more slowly.

"Oh my goodness, I'm sorry," Mary said. "Are you not from England? I thought you had just travelled up from London, but you do have a strange accent."

"I was born in China. My mother is Chinese, and my father was born in England," Aveling explained.

"I had no idea." Mary looked apologetic. "Things must be so strange. But don't worry, I can explain things as we go along. You must take after your father, as I don't think I have ever seen a Chinese girl – or, come to think about it, anybody – with eyes as green as yours." She smiled. "I would never have guessed you were half Chinese."

After breakfast, Mary showed Aveling to her classroom – a lower class than the one Mary was in. Immediately Mary approached the teacher and explained that Aveling's English was a little strange, then she headed off to her own class.

Aveling found herself in a room with fifteen other girls, who all seemed to be from mixed backgrounds, but learning anything that day was the furthest thing from her mind. She was still feeling confused about her situation and spent too much time just looking out of the window until the teacher tapped her on the shoulder.

"I have been watching you, young lady."

Aveling decided if she just responded in Chinese and shrugged her shoulders, perhaps the teacher would leave her alone. But she was mistaken.

"Nice try, young lady," said the teacher. "But I have already read your file. So when you are in my class, it will be English only. And if you don't understand anything, just ask."

To make things worse, she passed Aveling a test paper.

"You are lucky arriving on an exam day," she said sarcastically. "Now, girls, when you finish, bring the papers up to my desk then leave to go on break."

Aveling looked down at the exam paper and started to fill it in. She finished in less than fifteen minutes and took the paper over to the teacher's desk. She was met with a stern look in response, but placed the test sheet on the teacher's desk and left. With no idea where she was going, Aveling asked a girl she passed in the corridor how she could get outside to get some fresh air.

The rest of the day seemed to drag until she finally met back up with Mary after lessons. The other girl wanted to know where Aveling had been, as she hadn't seen her at lunch.

"What lunch?" asked Aveling.

"Oh Aveling," Mary said kindly, "you do have a lot to learn about living here in England."

The next day, she went to the same class, but no sooner had she sat down than there was a quiet knock on the door. When the headmistress entered the room, everybody stood and said in unison, "Morning, Mrs Dean."

"Good morning, girls. Now, if Aveling would like to join me, I have some good news." She smiled at Aveling. "Due to the results of your exam yesterday, I am moving you up to class seven." And she indicated that Aveling should follow her.

The new class seemed to be in the other wing of the school, but when Aveling entered the room, she was relieved to see it was the same class in which Mary was enrolled.

Over the next few weeks, time seemed to drag slowly, but she was fortunate to have Mary to talk to and ask for advice. Mary explained that the pupils in the school were all girls, and the only males were the headmistress's son, Robert, who was in his twenties, and the groundsman's son, Billy, who looked like he was still in his teens.

Most evenings Aveling liked to go to the library to do research. And although she invited Mary to join her, her roommate seemed to do well in her exams so she always declined. If she was honest, Aveling was relieved, as she always got more work done when she was on her own.

*

Mary often talked about her family, particularly her two brothers – Sam and Mark – and her boyfriend, Harry, who was her brother's best friend. She was looking forward to getting home to see them all at the end of that term.

Aveling, on the other hand, had no idea what she would be doing when the term ended. She was still living in hope that her dad would invite her home – wherever that was – or to meet her English grandmother, which Aveline was desperate to do.

Still preoccupied with her thoughts, she decided to head to her room earlier than usual to prepare for travelling to London if her father got in touch. But as she opened the door to the room, she froze. Two young men – Robert and Billy – were lying on Mary's bed with her, and all three were naked!

Aveling had never seen a naked man's body before, and she quickly stepped back into the corridor and shut the door. As she did so, she heard one of the boys saying, "Don't be shy! Come in and join us."

Her heart pounding, Aveling hurried down two flights of stairs to the foyer, where she sat down on a chair, struggling to process what she had just seen. A few minutes later the two boys came down and began tormenting her, asking her to join them next time.

But when Mary came down the stairs and saw the panic on Aveling's face, she ordered the boys to get out. When they seemed reluctant to leave, Mary told them if they ever wanted to see her again they should go.

When they had left, Mary asked Aveling to go back to up to their room with her. But once they were there, she played the whole thing down as if it was nothing out of the ordinary.

Aveling asked, "But I thought you liked your brother's friend Harry?"

Mary shrugged her shoulders. "Aveling, don't be such a prude, it was just a bit of fun."

By the last day of term, Aveling still hadn't heard from her father. So, it looked as though would have to spend the holidays on her own in the college.

Mary was aghast at the idea. She told Aveling she would be bored silly if she spent the holidays at the school, so she invited her to go with her to the family estate. As it was the only offer Aveling had, and she did not want to stay at the school on her own, she accepted. As they shared a room and had become friends, Aveling was sure Mary would look after her.

The following day Mary s father, who seemed friendly, picked them both up in a vehicle that looked like it belonged in a scrap yard – much to Mary's annoyance.

"Dad, why did you come in the old Land Rover? What will my friends think?"

But Aveling smiled and said, "At least your dad has picked you up. I have only seen my dad once since I left China, and back home only a few times in the past two years. And I haven't seen my mother for years."

After a while Mary's dad turned off the main road into a driveway leading up to a property that seemed just as big as the school. Aveling was wondering if he was perhaps the gardener or estate worker, until she heard Mary ask him how many guests would be joining them over the holidays.

When he said her brothers would be joining them, Mary asked if they were bringing their friend Harry. Every time Mary talked about him to Aveling, she always made it sound as though he was her soulmate. And she had made Aveling promise not to tell anyone about what she had seen back at the school.

It was a promise Aveling was happy to keep. In her view, talking about sex was disgusting and should only be discussed between husband and wife. But it certainly looked as though this was going to be a very interesting holiday.

CHAPTER 4: NEW FRIENDS

Mary's mother was at the door to greet them as they pulled into the driveway, and when Aveling stepped out of the Land Rover, she was welcomed by so many people, including the cook who wanted to know if she had any allergies.

Promising to introduce everyone to her later, Mary grabbed Aveling by the arm and dragged her upstairs to show her the room where she would be sleeping. It was huge, and Aveling felt lost in all that space, but she was happy to have been so welcomed and couldn't help but envy Mary such a lovely family.

Aveling's one concern was that she didn't have the right clothes to wear for dinner. But Mary soon solved that problem when she opened a closet to reveal so many outfits that it took Aveling's breath away. There were rows upon rows of garments in all colours and styles, and she wondered how Mary could possibly wear them when she was hardly ever there.

Mary explained that she often had friends to stay and liked to keep a full selection of outfits for them to share so they could be ready for any kind of event. She told Aveling to help herself to anything she fancied.

While they got ready for dinner, Mary explained that her brothers both worked on the estate. The eldest, Mark, lived in a cottage on the other side of the fields, while her younger brother Sam still lived at home and was just a few years older than her.

The first few days seemed to fly by, and Aveling quickly settled in, particularly as Mary was teaching her to ride. After the first week, Harry turned up to stay with Mark at the cottage. But although

Mary was always keen to ride across the fields just to see Harry, he barely said a word to them, and Aveling got the impression that he didn't share Mary's feelings.

On the last day of the holiday, a few days after Harry had left, Aveling was looking for Mary when she heard voices just off the hallway in the conservatory. As she neared the doorway, she overheard Mary saying something but couldn't make it out.

As a small child Aveling had repeatedly suffered hearing difficulties, but after years of going in and out of hospital for surgery, her hearing was almost perfect. During the difficult spell, though, she had learned how to lipread.

Peering through a crack in the door, she managed to make out Sam saying, "Keep your voices down in case anyone hears us."

Then she saw Mary asking if Aveling was a suitable candidate.

In response, both boys seemed excited. "Perfect," they both agreed.

Aveling headed back to her room to pack, but she was wary of asking Mary about the conversation in case she thought she had been spying on them.

The following morning, the girls were leaving to go back to school. As they prepared to climb into the back of the car, suddenly Mark grabbed hold of Aveling, spun her around, and gave her a hug and a kiss. As she was pushing him away, Sam took hold of her and held her tight, kissing her hard on the lips while she struggled to shake him off. When he finally let go, the look on his face made her feel like he was a mad dog and she was the bone.

Sensing her discomfort, Mary laughed. "Aveling, you are so silly. We always say goodbye with a kiss and hug. The boys don't mean anything by it."

Never having had any siblings, Aveling didn't know if this was normal behaviour, but for some reason Mary's brothers made her feel very uncomfortable.

On the long drive back to the school, Mary hardly spoke a word as she seemed too engrossed in her phone messages. Aveling, however, didn't own a mobile phone and had no-one to call, even if she'd had one.

When they returned to the school and were settling back into their room, Aveling decided to ask Mary about the conversation she had overheard with the two brothers. Although Mary had been the only one to help her at the school and they shared a room, Aveling still wasn't sure she could trust the other girl completely.

"Oh! I thought I saw you standing in the doorway, but you should have asked me then," Mary responded. "It is no big deal. I was going to wait till we returned at the end of this term, but Sam has always loved art and was hoping you would model for him."

Aveling didn't know what to say to that. She did not want to distrust Mary, but some things just did not add up, making Aveling more cautious.

*

Halfway into the term, Aveling was just changing class one day when she was pulled aside by a girl she didn't know. Apologising for what she was about to say, the girl explained that when she had been new to the school, Mary had offered to share a room then invited her back to her family home.

The girl said that Mary's brother Sam had turned on the charm and promised to make her a top model if she took off her clothes and allowed him to paint her in the nude. Naively, she had agreed and was taken to Mark's cottage, believing it would just be her and Sam present.

The room was already set up with an easel and art equipment just in front of the window, the girl said, and Sam put her at ease and talked her into removing her clothes.

But as she was lying on the couch naked, the girl explained that Mark and Mary arrived. With tears in her eyes, she went on to tell Aveling that both brothers raped her while Mary, who was also naked, watched.

"When I thought they had finished with me, I tried to get dressed, but Mary said they had not finished with me yet. She pushed me back down on the couch, saying it was her turn, then she then began to stroke and fondle me between my legs. Then," the girl explained haltingly, "Mark, who by then had another erection, had sex with his own sister as I was forced to watch. Mary kept saying, 'Now this is how you please a man.'

"When I said I would call the police, Sam pointed to a camera on a shelf. They told me if I said anything to anybody, they would release the film to the internet for everyone to see, and they would send a copy of the recording to my parents."

The girl explained that a few weeks later she had been sent a copy of the recording from one of her family's friends, who was in his sixties. "He asked if I would entertain him and a few friends, and said if I declined, he was willing to send a copy of the recording to my parents."

As she had been a virgin before that night and had not been on any sort of contraception, she had been shocked to discover she was pregnant. Too afraid to tell her parents, instead she told them she was going on a school trip but had gone to have an abortion.

When she returned to school later, following complications, the girl said, things deteriorated further. She discovered that her parents had received a call from the school asking why she was not back for the start of the new term, telling them there had been no school trip.

Devastated, afraid, and unable to face anybody, she had attempted to take her own life.

Engrossed in their conversation, both girls jumped in surprise when the school bell suddenly sounded. But as the girl started to walk away, Aveling pulled her back.

"Why didn't your parents go to the police?" she asked.

"They did," the girl replied, "but on the recording all you could see was me removing my own clothes and lying down on the couch naked. The easel and paints had been too far right, so the camera didn't show them. They had also cut the tape just after Mark had sex with me, so when the police and legal team said that all they could see was me removing my own clothes, they told my father that I had been asking for it, and if we went to court we would lose." The girl's voice broke with emotion as she went on, "Father had to think of the family's name and reputation."

As the girl walked away, Aveling realised her own instincts had been right all along, and there was no way she would ever be going back to Mary's home again.

*

After the last class of the day, Aveling decided she did not want to return to her room, so she found a quiet part of the gardens where she could sit and finish her homework. She hadn't been there long when Mary found her.

"Hi, what have you been up to? It took me ages to find you."

Aveling was still trying to convince herself that Mary would never set up a schoolfriend, wondering if perhaps the girl had gone to the cottage for Sam to paint her and things had just got out of hand. But her memory of finding Mary naked in their room with two young men was still fresh in her mind.

As they were chatting, the girl Aveling had been talking to passed by and glanced across at Mary with an evil look on her face.

Immediately, Mary shouted across the lawn, "What's your problem?"

Aveling asked, "Why are you shouting at that girl? Do you know her?"

"That is the little liar who tried to damage my family's reputation," Mary replied angrily.

Aveling asked what she meant, but Mary went silent. When she asked again, Mary snapped, "That's the little bitch who seduced my brother then told everybody he had raped her, when my brother would never do such a thing."

The encounter with the girl was never mentioned again, and some weeks later when the girls were nearing another school break, Mary invited Aveling to join her again at the family home.

This time, Aveling was quick to refuse. She explained that her family were coming up from London to visit her during the holidays, but she knew by the expression on Mary's face that she did not believe her. After all, she was well aware that Aveling had never received a letter or phone call in all the months she had been there.

On the day she was preparing to leave for the holiday, Mary suddenly asked Aveling, "Has that girl said something to you?

I promise you everything she says is all lies. I told you, neither of my brothers would ever do such a thing."

Aveling was torn and did not know what to believe. Mary had been so welcoming when she had first arrived at the school and needed a friend, and the thought of spending a week at school when all the other girls were away didn't appeal to her. But on the other hand, she felt uneasy around Mary's two brothers.

Mary went on, "It's ok, you don't have to worry about my brothers being around. It's the summer fair, and my brothers will be at the showground to show the best animals. Dad always says if we can get more gold awards, we can sell more beef. And as the showground is so far away, my brothers will be staying over with my uncle."

Sensing her uncertainty, Mary grabbed Aveling's bag and told her to pack quickly.

"Come on, slow coach, we don't want to keep Dad waiting."

And within minutes, and with her head still swirling, Aveling found herself packed and in the car heading to Mary's home once again.

CHAPTER 5: LIES

Everything that holiday was bliss. Every day Mary took Aveling horse riding, the weather was great, the girls had great fun together, and there was no sign of the brothers all week.

On the night before they were due to return to school, Aveling was packing up her things when she realised she could not find her comb. Remembering she had lent it to Mary, she headed along the corridor to Mary's room, stopping outside the door when she realised the girl was on the phone.

"It's ok, Sam, I have told Dad we don't need to go back to school for another day. So when you get back, don't come up here to the house. Go directly to the cottage and I will get Aveling over there for a last horse ride."

Mary had the phone on speaker, as she was still applying makeup in the hope that Harry was coming to see her before they returned to school. But it was what Aveling heard next that sent shivers down her spine.

Mary was laughing. "Don't worry. It's your turn this weekend. Mark took the last little virgin, and I know how much you like Aveling."

"Well," Sam could be heard clearly on the speaker, "she does have the most amazing black hair, and those green eyes of hers just turn me on. I get so excited thinking about her. Are you sure she won't cause any problems like the last girl?"

"Stop panicking," Mary replied. "I have got it all worked out, and remember it only got messy last time because the stupid little bitch got pregnant. Just think about all the other little virgins

I have got for you and Mark over the years, and how much money we all made. Don't worry about Aveling. I will slip a contraceptive pill and Rohypnol into her drink just before we leave for the cottage, so stay calm. And remember, you promised I could film it all myself, because I have promised Harry a weekend treat. I know Harry is just as fascinated with Aveling as you are, so stop worrying."

"No, sis, don't do that," Sam urged. "I know Harry well, and he will blow his top if he sees Aveling on video. You know he has never approved with what we do, even when we told him the girls were all willing. Remember when we asked him just to post a video on the internet when our computer went down? He told Mark we must be crazy. You might think that because you and Harry have never had sex, he would accept seeing Aveling on the internet – even if we insisted she was willing. But, honestly, Harry would never believe us."

"Stop right there!" Mary replied angrily. "I have tried everything to get that man to have sex with me, but he just keeps saying not until we get married. But I think if he sees her on tape, I can finally get him to give it up."

"It won't work, sis." Sam was adamant.

"Well, I need the money," Mary replied. "I will be hiking up the price on this one before I launch it on the internet, because this is my last year at school, so we need to make as much money out of this film as we can. And with Aveling's looks, we will make a killing." She paused briefly then added, "See you later, brother. And don't worry. I promise you will enjoy what I have planned for you. See you both at the cottage."

Aveling leaned against the landing wall for support. She felt sick and angry that she had been so stupid as to trust Mary and fall for her lies. In a moment of panic, she hurried back to her room, determined to pack her things and get the hell out of there.

But just she reached her room, she could hear Mary walking across the landing. Aveling grabbed a book and pretended to be reading.

"Hi Aveling." Mary breezed into the room with a smile. "I thought we could go down and hang around the stables."

"Sorry, Mary, but I must finish this book so that I will be ready for the maths exam. It's one of the subjects I have to pass."

"Ok, not a problem. See you later."

Knowing this would be her only chance to escape, Aveling watched through the window as Mary left the house and headed for the stables. She felt bad at leaving without seeing Mary's parents, who had been so lovely and welcoming. So, she scribbled a short note to leave on the hall table, explaining that she'd received a phone call from her father saying he needed her back in London and had called a taxi.

But as Aveling slipped quietly out of the front door, she didn't realise that the note had blown down behind the table, out of sight.

It was already late in the afternoon, and Aveling believed if she called a taxi to such a remote place, it would take too long to get there. She was also worried that if she took the long walk down the driveway, she might bump into Mary's brothers returning home.

Believing it was her best chance to get away, she opted to take a pathway she had never been down before. As she started to walk, rain began to fall and got heavier, slowing her down and making walking difficult. Soaked through and exhausted, Aveling glanced at her watch and realised she must have been walking for several hours.

Suddenly she heard the sound of a car engine getting closer. She scanned what she could of the woods and land around her, but it was so hard to see in the dark. All she knew was that she would be in danger if they saw her, so she had to hide.

As the fear began to build in her stomach, a hand went over her mouth and someone whispered, "Get down and don't make a sound."

Aveling wanted to scream, but the hand was tightly over her mouth as she was dragged down behind a huge pile of stone. Not far away she could hear the car engine stopping and muffled voices – one of which was Mary's – calling her name.

As the car moved slowly off again, she struggled to break free but the hand stayed firmly over her mouth. "Aveling, it's ok, it's me. Harry."

Aveling had only met Harry on a few occasions, usually when Mary was draping herself all over him. But his voice seemed calm. And having overheard Mary tell her brother that she'd never had sex with Harry, Aveling thought it would be safe to trust him. So, she stopped struggling.

Harry slowly removed his hand but stayed directly behind her. He whispered that they should stay put as the road ended just a few hundred yards ahead, at a quarry, so the car would have to turn and pass them again. This time, though, it drove past without stopping.

Aveling felt a huge sigh of relief. She turned around to face Harry and could make out his face smiling, despite the dark.

"I live just past the back field. No-one goes over there anymore, so you can stay there tonight." He frowned. "Why are you hiding from them? Did you not tell them you were leaving?"

Aveling explained that she had left a note on the hall table, so couldn't understand why they were out looking for her. When she explained her reason for not calling a taxi, he agreed it would have taken too long to get there.

"It's late now, so stay at my place tonight, then let's work out what you would like to do in the morning."

Aveling breathed a sigh of relief. The rain was heavy and the wind was howling, so she nodded her head, and Harry took her by the hand.

"Best stay close to the house," he explained, "as it's a bit dangerous around here, with the wild animals and being so close to the quarry."

When they reached Harry's home, all the lights were out. As they made their way inside in the dark, he suggested it would be best if they only put the light on up on the landing. He explained that if the car went past and saw his lights on, they would know he was home and stop by.

"On second thoughts," he suggested, "it might be better if I rang the house and tell them I saw you waiting for a taxi and gave you a lift to the railway station. That will stop them all looking for you."

Aveling agreed. "That sounds like a good idea. I don't want them to find me."

Harry showed Aveling upstairs to a back bedroom. "You can sleep here," he said. "You're soaked through. Let me run you a bath." He moved to a landing cupboard and pulled out several fresh towels.

It was only when Aveling put down her backpack that she realised she had no clean clothes with her,

"Don't worry. I will get you some things that should fit. You have a good soak, and I'll make us some hot tea."

As she soaked in the bath, Harry knocked on the door. "Is it ok if I just open the door a little, and drop these clothes in for you?"

"Ok," Aveling answered, a little nervously. But to her relief, Harry quickly dropped the clothes onto the floor then closed the door again.

When she returned to her bedroom, she found a hot cup of tea had been left on the bedside cupboard. As she glanced at the clock on the table, which showed 1am, she heard Harry outside the door calling goodnight.

Aveling was exhausted, but she did feel safe. Mary had told her that she and Harry had never had sex because he wanted to stay a virgin until he got married. Snuggling under the duvet, Aveling rested her head on the pillow and fell fast asleep.

A few hours later, just as dawn was breaking, she heard someone open her bedroom door. Half asleep, she opened her eyes very slightly and, with the daylight creeping through the curtains, saw it was Harry.

"What's wrong?" she asked sleepily.

But without answering, he sat on the bed and lowered his lips to kiss her.

"Get off!" she snapped, trying to sit up.

But he pulled the covers off, pushed her back down, and climbed on top of her. Ignoring her screams, he pulled up her t-shirt and ripped off her knickers. Then he forced himself inside her, deeper and deeper, while she screamed in pain, tears streaming down her face.

She couldn't believe she had run from the danger back at the house only to find herself being raped by someone who had promised to help her.

When he finally finished, he got up, adjusted his own clothes, then left without saying a word. A few moments later, she heard his bedroom door close.

Ignoring her pain, Aveling got up and put on some of her still-damp clothes then made her way downstairs and outside. She was immediately hit by a wall of rain, but she left the door wide open as she walked away with her few belongings in her backpack.

Trudging down the quiet dirt road, she felt numb. How could he do that to her when Mary must have been after him for months to have sex?

She hadn't been walking long when she saw an old empty building and decided to go inside to get out of the rain. Stumbling against one of the walls, she slipped down into a heap on the floor and started sobbing.

Suddenly she remembered her grandmother's words. She slipped her hand inside the backpack until her fingers felt the silk strip, and she began to pull it free of the jumbled mess inside. At that moment she knew exactly what she needed to do.

Aveling felt it was the only way to end the pain that seemed so unbearable. She tied a small stone into the corner of the silk, then threw it over a high beam that looked like it was the only thing still holding the building up.

Looking around, she saw a broken box. She dragged it over then stood on it, wrapping the silk around her neck. Without any hesitation, she kicked the box away.

The next thing she remembered was lying on the damp, cold floor. Aveling tried to open her eyes only to close them again, wondering if she was still alive.

She tried to move but felt no sensation in her limbs. Her voice deserted her, convincing her she must be dead. Then she felt a pain she had never felt before; something was pushing her harder and harder, firmly keeping her from moving,

She felt like her body no longer belonged to her. But just for a few seconds, her eyes opened and she made out a face a few inches above hers. It left her with a sense of an angel, with bright blue eyes, blond hair, and a look of serenity. For one brief moment, she thought, *Angel. No, devil.*

The next thing she remembered was waking up in a hospital ward. The noise was overwhelming as doctors, nurses, patients, people pushing tea trollies, all seemed to be talking over each other.

Aveling tried to get up out of the bed only to be pushed gently back down again.

"Now, young lady, where do you think you are going?"

A man in a white coat seemed to be talking to her, but everything just seemed to be a jumble of words. As she focused her eyes around the room, she heard a nurse ask for her name and details.

But when Aveling tried to speak, her voice failed her.

"It's ok, young lady," the doctor told her kindly, "you have damaged your vocal cords, but just give yourself some more time."

CHAPTER 6: BETRAYED

Over the next few days, the nurses would regularly bring her a pen and paper to write down her details, but at that point Aveling had decided to tell them nothing. What was the point? she reasoned to herself. After all, her grandmother was still in China; her father – well, at that point she didn't know for sure but she believed he was still with his new family out of the country, and it had been months since she had any contact with him; and her mother had not been in touch with her for many years.

Aveling knew she had a grandmother still living in England – her father's mother – but had only seen her when she was incredibly young, when the grandmother visited them at the Embassy in China.

Still wrestling with confusing feelings of guilt, shame, and fear, she was surprised when a nurse approached her carrying a huge bunch of flowers.

"Well now, miss," she said with a big smile. "Someone is thinking about you."

Over the next few days, the flowers kept arriving, and the message on the card always said the same thing: *Get well and come home soon. Lots of hugs and kisses, your loving brother Harry.*

Aveling was furious and told the nurse she did not have a brother. But although she insisted they threw the flowers away, the staff never listened, and each day she would see the flowers all over the ward.

She knew he would be getting a kick out of playing with her mind, but she was determined she would have her revenge. As each bunch of flowers arrived, Aveling's resolve strengthened to make Harry,

Mark, Sam, and Mary suffer, once she was discharged. She wanted to repay them for all the other girls' lives they had destroyed. And in Harry's case, she would make him eat his bloody flowers, one petal at a time.

*

Once her condition improved, Aveling was moved to a newer wing of the hospital and put in a room of her own. She was relieved not to have to share, and it was much quieter than the old ward, but the room was locked each night at ten, and if she needed the toilet Aveling had to press a bell and wait for help to come to the room.

Aveling was hoping if the female guard left her alone maybe she could escape, but there were bars at all the windows and it felt more like a prison than a hospital,

During the first few nights alone, Aveling would empty her backpack onto her bed and open up the small velvet bag with three pieces of jade. It was a reminder of her grandmother back in China and had become the most important thing in her life. She had no idea what had happened to the nine yards of silk, so for the time being the contents of that bag kept her focused on getting out of there and taking her revenge. To her mind, the jade had once belonged to a queen, and if she had managed to escape death then so could Aveling.

After a few weeks, Aveling was assigned what she would call a shrink. At their first meeting, she never said a word. Even though her voice had returned, it seemed to have changed and sounded softer and quieter. Sitting in his office, she just stared out of the window, watching the trees outside blowing in the wind, while the man on the opposite side of the desk made notes. He did not say a lot, but every now and then he would look up from his paperwork and smile. "When you are ready, young lady, I am here to help."

On her fourth visit, the doctor was standing by the door waiting for her. "Now," he said, "I don't believe you don't know who you are, and I don't believe this act of yours of playing dumb. So cut it out and let's get down to business."

They sat down on either side of the desk, and the man continued to ask questions. But Aveling remained silent. The name on his desk plate said Dr Tommy Bellson, and Aveling reckoned he must be in his early thirties, maybe a little older. With slim build and a goatee beard, he had an old-fashioned look, but she was sure it was all part of his persona to make him look more like a head doctor than a shrink. As far as she was concerned, all men were monsters.

Aveling knew she had been receiving medication for several weeks which made her very tired all the time, so she asked the doctor if he could stop insisting she took them. She also demanded to know when she could be discharged, claiming she was fine and would be much better when she was released.

But Dr Bellson did not seem convinced. "You need to start answering my questions, young lady. And as you don't appear to know anybody outside, where will you go? Where will you stay?"

The same conversation carried on for a few more weeks, each time she saw him, with both of them becoming frustrated at the repeated questions and answers. In the end, all she would tell him was her first name.

After their latest session, Dr Bellson returned to his family home, where his grandmother was sitting in her office. He'd never had any problems in getting any of his female patients to talk. His confident and caring manner had always worked before, but not with Aveling.

As always, Tommy turned to his grandmother for advice, as she had been a GP for years and had often handled a few patients with problems for the court authorities.

That evening, he began to explain that he had a patient he just could not get through to. His grandmother listened carefully, only interrupting when he mentioned the girl's name.

"What did you call her?" she asked.

"Aveling."

"Well, that's strange. Do you remember, when you were studying, I told you how I had a patient with problems called Aveling."

"Ah, I thought the name seemed familiar," he agreed. "Wasn't she the one who escaped from the supermarket, right under the noses of the two escorting police officers?"

"That's right. Can you describe your Aveling?"

"Yes. She's seventeen, slim build, with jet black hair and the most piercing green eyes. I know I shouldn't say this, but I am just drawn to her like a moth to a flame. I just want to help her."

His grandmother frowned. "You know better than that, Tommy. You need to hand her over to another doctor if she is going to be a problem." She paused, deep in thought. "I remember my Aveling had a similar built-in man magnet that would just pull in any man with her bright green eyes. Like you have already said, like moths to a flame."

"Do you think they could be related?"

"I don't see how, but it's possible. When I used the recording machine for the first time, I would allow my Aveling to go into the back office and just speak in her own time about whatever was troubling her. Even though she escaped, I still like to think I helped her."

"Have you ever heard from her again, Grandma?"

His grandmother shook her head. "No. She is still wanted by the police, and so many years have passed that I don't think I will ever see or hear from her again."

Tommy looked thoughtful. "I know this sounds crazy, but with such a unique name and similarities, can we give it a try to find her?"

His grandmother shrugged. "I don't think I would know where to start. As I say, she is still wanted by the police, assuming she is still alive. No, Tommy, I doubt it's possible."

"Look, Grandma, at this stage I haven't got any other ideas to help my Aveling, and we cannot just let her go, as I don't think she will last a day on the streets. How about we put a small advert in the newspapers just saying 'Aveling, I need you. Dr Valerie'?" Valerie was his grandmother's name.

"Well, normally I would say you would be wasting your money, but if you are keeping this girl just because you have started to have feelings for her, you need to stop now. If you are just trying to help the girl, then fair enough. I do know what it's like to have a patient that makes you feel helpless, but so much time has passed that I doubt my Aveling is still alive, and if she sees the advert whether she would answer."

The next day, Dr Bellson wasted no time in sending an email to the advertising department of several local newspapers and even a national paper with the simple message: 'Aveling, help. Dr Valerie.' He asked for the ad to be printed postcard size and added his grandmother's mobile number.

*

Back at work the following day, Tommy started to doubt himself. He knew it was a long shot to place the advertisement, but he felt he just had to do something to help his young patient.

When his mobile phone rang in the middle of the morning, it caught him off guard, and he was surprised to see the caller ID show his grandmother.

"You won't believe it, Tommy," she said excitedly, "but it's worked. I received a call just a few minutes ago from Aveling! She didn't say much over the phone, but I have made an appointment for you to meet with her later this evening at the old mill. I know that seems like a strange place to meet, but I guess she is still nervous. I'll text you the details."

"That's great, Grandma. I will let you know how it goes."

That evening, on his way to meet his grandmother's Aveling, Tommy reflected on how cloak and dagger the meeting seemed. It was already quite dark when he arrived, but he could just make out a hooded figure stepping out of the old building.

As he got closer and she came into focus, he saw a petite woman dressed all in black.

"Well now, young man, I take it you are a relative of Dr Valerie, and you have some questions for me."

"I don't know if you can help," Tommy began nervously, "but I have someone who needs help, and she is also called Aveling."

"What does she look like?" the cloaked woman asked.

"She is seventeen, with jet black hair, speaks with a strange accent, and has the most beautiful green eyes I have ever seen. Actually, she is the only person I have ever met who has green eyes that bright."

At that moment, he looked directly into the woman's eyes and gasped as he saw hers were the same shade of green. *Surely*, he thought, *there could be no doubt the two women were related somehow?*

"I was talking with my grandmother, and she told me your story," he continued.

"Hopefully not all my story," she replied calmly. "I do have a granddaughter who fits your description, but I was under the assumption she was still in China. How and where can I meet your Aveling?"

"I work in the hospital, and she is still being held in the ward for people under suicide watch," he explained.

"Has she told you anything? If it is my granddaughter and she is back in this country, that bloody son of mine has a lot to answer for. I could have met her when she arrived, if he had told me."

Frowning, she took out her mobile phone and punched in a number. In the quiet of the evening, Tommy could hear that the call was answered by a woman who confirmed she was Carol, the new wife of Madam Aveling's son.

In a strong Yorkshire accent, Madam Aveling insisted Carol put her son on the phone immediately, and Tommy realised this was not a woman to be messed with.

Switching phone to speaker, Madam Aveling demanded to know where, when, and how her granddaughter had ended up in England without her even being informed. Her son, who sounded nervous, gave the name of the boarding school, after which he was subjected to an angry tirade from his mother.

"You take yourself off to the British Embassy in bloody China, then you marry a Chinese girl without even inviting me and your father to your wedding. And after your daughter is born, I receive a Christmas card once a bloody year with a photo of baby Aveling, if I am bloody lucky." Her voice was growing louder and louder.

"As Aveling's been growing up, with more and more promises that you would bring her back to visit me, I've only had a few phone calls a year, telling me you are well and everything is good with you and your daughter. And when I was lucky enough to get an email, there was always an attachment asking for money! Just why did you need so much extra money when the girl was in a private school that, I might remind you, I was paying for.

"Just what the hell do you do with the rest of the money? Ah, that's right, you've just got a new wife, so I guess you need the money for her." With that, Madam Aveling slammed the phone down.

Taking a deep breath, she tucked her phone away then turned to Tommy and demanded he take her to the hospital. As it was so late, he would have to enter via the outside security gates protecting the new wing. He felt a little nervous trying to get her in at that time of night, past the guards, but he did not want to argue with this woman. And, after all, he had contacted her first.

For the first time, he realised why his grandmother had warned him about the outcome of dealing with Madam Aveling.

CHAPTER 7: ON THE RUN

Refusing to travel in Tommy's car, Madam Aveling informed her that her driver would follow him on the journey to the hospital. By the time they arrived, most of the indoor lighting had been turned to night mode.

After explaining to the security guards that he was dealing with an urgent case, Dr Bellson produced his identity card and first his, then Madam Aveling's car, were allowed through.

As she got out of her car, Tommy noticed she immediately pulled her scarf high across her face. He remembered then that this woman had been in a high security prison before someone had planned her escape. *But*, he wondered, *why was she still hiding herself?*

As he began to question whether he had done the right thing by placing the advert, they climbed the two flights of stairs to Aveling's room. But when he unlocked the door, the room was empty!

Madam looked as if she was about to kill someone, and he was in the direct firing line. But he was just dumbstruck. His mind was in overdrive; he had never lost a patient before. How on earth had young Aveling escaped?

Madam Aveling was angry, but she also felt trapped and uncomfortable with so many cameras everywhere, and she raised the scarf even further up her face.

She knew that Aveling, if she was anything like her, would have found a way to escape if she wanted to. But it seemed amazing that she could just disappear from a high security ward. It didn't help that Dr Bellson's face was a blank and he seemed at a loss to know what to do.

After a few minutes, he gathered his thoughts and they both headed downstairs to talk to the security team. Madam Aveling couldn't imagine where her granddaughter would go if she escaped, and if she had been taken out by force, she wanted to know by whom and how.

It hadn't occurred to Dr Bellson that Aveling had been kidnapped; he had just assumed she had escaped. So, when one of the security guards suggested running back the CCTV cameras, he was only too happy to agree.

The cameras outside picked up a man parking his car, but the registration plate was covered in mud so it was impossible to read. The next camera showed him entering the hospital wing, where he appeared to sign in as Aveling's brother. It was clear to see on the camera that the man was wearing a disguise, so both Tommy and Madam Aveling were shocked at how easily he had got past security.

He was taken to the visitor's room, where they saw him ask for two cups of tea. When the tea arrived, the camera clearly showed the man putting something into one of the cups. Then he put the two cups on the table and asked if he could quickly use the toilet.

The camera outside Aveling's room recorded her being taken by the nursing staff to meet her visitor. But it was obvious on the recording that she wanted to return to her room. And when the nursing staff told her to be brave and that he was only there to help her, they could hear Aveling continually saying she did not have a brother.

Back in the visitor's room, the recording showed Aveling being ushered in and told that her visitor had gone to the bathroom but had ordered her a nice cup of tea. Still unsure about what was going on, Aveling looked a little dazed but sat down and began to drink her tea.

As she was finishing her drink, her so-called brother returned to the room, and her head could clearly be seen on the camera, slowly dropping onto her chest.

At that point, the 'brother' told the nurse on duty that Aveling had a little headache and he asked if he could borrow one of the wheelchairs to take her outside to the new gardens for a little fresh air.

As there were other visitors in the hospital at that time, and the tearoom was busy, no-one noticed when she did not return. But Dr Bellson and Madam Aveling saw quite clearly on the camera that the man pushed her wheelchair out of the entrance unchallenged by security staff and to his vehicle. A camera in the car park showed her being lifted into his car.

As they watched, shocked at how easy it had been to take Aveling from the hospital, the security guard showing them the recordings picked up the phone and called the police to report a kidnapping.

Before Dr Bellson could say any more, Madam Aveling began making her way out of the hospital, determined to make herself scarce before the police arrived. Furious at the hospital's blunder and the fact that no-one had checked their patient actually had a brother, she headed for her car and immediately rang her son for information on the school where the girl had been enrolled.

As her driver pulled away from the hospital, she was on the phone to the boarding school. The first person who answered the phone was the night security guard, who dismissed her request to speak to the headmistress and suggested she call back in the morning,

But she informed him that one of the pupils had been kidnapped, and if he did not get the head on the phone immediately, she would get him sacked. As she held on, Madam Aveling could hear sirens in the background and decided not to hang around any longer. She also knew officers would be sent to the boarding school, dashing her hopes of getting there first.

NINE YARDS OF SILK AND THREE PIECES OF JADE

Hanging up the call, she instructed her driver to put his foot down and they sped along country lanes, arriving at the school as the parking lot filled up with police cars. She ordered her driver to park at the far end of the parking area, believing the vehicle would just be out of camera range.

Now that Dr Bellson had Aveling's full details and knew that her father was a diplomat, it was guaranteed that the police would immediately try to track the girl's last movements before she ended up at the hospital. Madam Aveling was pretty sure they would also be sending a ransom team to Aveling's father's home to man the phones for contact from the kidnapper.

She was pretty sure, though, that this was not a kidnapping for money. In her view, any man who would go to the trouble to kidnap the girl from a locked-down hospital had other ideas.

She sat in her car for what seemed the longest of time, only finally climbing out when the last of the police cars left. The school had some very important pupils, including daughters of diplomats and royal families around the world. So when she finally got to speak to the headmistress, the woman informed her that the police had told her to not speak to anyone.

Speaking very calmly, Madam Aveling told her, "I assure you, I am not just anyone, and if you don't give me the answers to my questions now, I will have this school emptied before the end of the month when I inform the girls' parents just how slack your rules and security are. I can also assure you that you will not be reopening when I have your fire certificate, safety certificate, and insurance, all cancelled. By the time I finish with you, you will need to get my permission to work as a street cleaner."

The headmistress was used to dealing with difficult parents and would not normally allow anybody to speak to her in that manner. But before she could reply, the school security officer tapped her on the shoulder and whispered something into her ear. Madam

Aveling could not hear the conversation, but by lip reading she guessed the security officer must have seen the badge on the front of her car .

Although she had kept her car out of the sight of the cameras, it had not escaped the attention of the guard, whom she recognised as having worked for her husband many years before. He knew she was not a lady to be messed with. And after he finished whispering his message, the head teacher's attitude changed and she was only too willing to provide Madam Aveling with the answers to every question.

During the questioning, she learned that her granddaughter had left school at the end of term to spend the holiday with her best friend Mary Glenhall at her family's country estate. Armed with the information and address, Madam Aveling went back to her car and headed off to the Glenhall Estate.

As the car made its way up the long driveway, the morning sun was just rising and the estate was only just coming alive with the arrival of workers. Madam Aveling hammered on the front door of the huge gothic building, and informed the housekeeper in no uncertain terms that she was not leaving until she got answers from the family.

A few minutes later, Mary's father appeared bleary-eyed in his dressing gown and instructed the housekeeper to get his daughter out of bed. When she joined them in the hallway, Mary seemed to have answers for ever question, and claimed that as far as she was concerned Aveling had gone to spend time with her father in London.

Madam Aveling did not believe one word that Mary said. Having learned to handle questioning by police and courts when she was young, Madam Aveling knew all the tricks and knew that everyone had a 'tell' when they were lying. In Mary's case, Madam Aveling identified that the girl was good at hiding the truth but would twist her hair when she was telling lies.

When Mary was asked if young Aveling knew anyone else on the estate, the girl paused. And before she could reply, the housekeeper interrupted to say that the girl knew both of Mary's brothers, and Mary's boyfriend Harry, who lived at the far end of the estate near the old quarry.

Spotting the angry look which Mary gave the housekeeper, Madam Aveling persisted with her questioning, asking who would have been the last person to have seen her granddaughter. Again, the housekeeper jumped in to reply before Mary, saying that Harry had given her a lift to the station.

Madam Aveling was convinced that Mary was hiding something, and she was determined to keep a close eye on the girl. But first, she needed to speak to this boy Harry, even if Mary called to warn him she was heading his way.

Her driver set off in the direction of Harry s house, but just as they were getting close, they were overtaken by a police car which pulled in just in front of an old farmhouse. Madam Aveling told the driver, James, to pull back and park up between two trees, where they waited and watched. Harry s house was well set back from the road, and after a brief time the police left.

James knew how to tune into the police radio bandwaves, so they listened as the officers leaving Harry's house reported that he had claimed not to have seen Aveling since he gave her a lift to the railway station. Another officer said they would need to pull all the security footage from the railway station, which would prove if Harry was telling the truth.

As she and her driver had been up all night, Madam Aveling told him to drive to the next village, where they booked into a hotel. She needed a rest before taking any more steps to find her granddaughter.

Even though the police had left Harry's house after a very brief visit, she had a feeling they were onto something so she would need to tread very carefully. Perhaps they wanted to check the station tapes before deciding if they should get a warrant to search his house. A warrant wasn't something Madam Aveling would need, though. Not when James was with her.

If her instinct was right and Harry knew more than he was letting on, she was pretty sure it was pointless to question him right now. She would return later and keep the farmhouse under observation. But first, she and her driver needed to get some sleep.

*

By listening to the police radio conversations, Madam Aveling knew that the officers did not have a registration number for the car that had kidnapped her granddaughter, but they knew the make and model and that Harry owned a similar car. However, there was no car parked on the road or driveway of his cottage in the morning when they returned, even though James had snooped around and could see Harry was inside.

For his part, Harry was no fool. When he'd kidnapped Aveling from the hospital, he had taken her to a derelict building at the end of a field just before the quarry, and which had once been used by quarry workers. No-one ever went there anymore, and it was large enough to park his car inside.

That morning, while Madam Aveling and James were watching the farmhouse, he slipped out of the back door and made his way across the fields to the deserted building. When he got there, Aveling was sleeping, her hands and feet bound with cable ties. And even when he tried to wake her, she was still groggy from the drugs he had given her.

As he pulled her up into a sitting position, Aveling started to cry, demanding to know why he was doing this. He kept saying he had not meant to hurt her and trotted out a pathetic excuse that he must have been sleepwalking, as it was only when he saw the blood on his bedsheets the following morning that he realised what must have happened.

Harry kept saying how sorry he was, he was going to put everything right, and he even told her he loved her and wanted to marry her. But Aveling needed to understand why he had raped her when Mary had been only too happy to have sex with him.

Grabbing the top of her arms and squeezing firmly, he snapped, "Have you never heard the saying that if you lay down with dogs, you get up with fleas? There was no way in this world I would ever sleep with that filthy bitch."

And as he pushed Aveling angrily back down, he muttered that she didn't have to worry about catching any disease because he was a virgin – as if that would make her feel better.

Trying to clear her mind and stay calm, Aveling asked to use the toilet. At some point during the night, she had lost control of her bladder and wet herself. Cold and still wet, she begged him to take her back to the house to get something dry to wear.

Harry could see she was wet, but he knew it wasn't safe to take her to his house yet. He told her if she finished all of the drink he had brought her, he would go and collect some dry clothes for her. Pushing the drink between her lips, he kept repeating that he would look after her, using force to hold her head still when she tried to turn away.

Aveling realised that he must have put more drugs in the drink, so she kept trying to knock the cup from his hand, but she was too weak to stop him. Within minutes she again lost all feeling in her legs and her eyes slowly closed.

When she awoke, it was dark outside, so she realized she must have been asleep most of the day. Certain that no-one would miss her, Aveling was slowly losing her will to live.

CHAPTER 8: TRAPPED

As she shook her head trying to come to her senses, Aveling realised Harry had returned. When she felt him pulling off her skirt, she believed he was going to put on clean clothes, but he placed a thick blanket on the floor and rolled her onto it, her hands and feet still tied with cable ties,

As he cut the ties around her feet, she thought he was going to release her hands, too. But instead he ripped off her knickers, forced her legs apart, then climbed on top of her and raped her again. Aveling tried to scream, but he immediately grabbed the stained knickers, still smelling of urine, from the floor and pushed them into her mouth.

With her hands still trapped behind her back, she struggled to break free, causing the cable ties to cut her skin. Once he'd finished, he removed the knickers from her mouth and threw them away, telling her she would not need them anymore. It was then Aveling saw him taking more cable ties from his bag, and she realised he intended keeping her there for his own sexual satisfaction.

If she had any chance of getting out of there, she knew she could not let him tie her legs again. So, she waited for the moment when he turned his back to her, then pulled herself up and bolted out of the entrance.

Still feeling the effects of the drugs, she wasn't quick enough and he caught up with her easily and grabbed her by her hair. He screamed at her that she was pregnant with his baby, and he wanted to keep her safe and look after them both.

Stunned at his outburst and sure he must be lying, Aveling continued to struggle with him, managing to bash her head off his nose, causing it to bleed. But the injury only made him more angry and he slapped her hard across the face.

As he pulled a tissue from his pocket to stop the bleeding, Aveling started to walk backwards. Her hands were still tied and she was still unsteady on her feet, so she had no idea how close to the side of the quarry she was. And by the time Harry realised and screamed at her to stop, she had fallen over the quarry edge.

Without her hands to enable her to grab onto anything, she fell over halfway down the side of the deep quarry before coming to an abrupt stop on a ledge. The pain was unbearable, and as she lay helpless, looking up at the stars in the sky, she thought she could hear Harry shouting.

Lying there, still naked from the waist down, it was cold. But now the pain had stopped, and she realised that the face she had thought was an angel when she had been cut down from the nine yards of silk, had been Harry's face. The realisation made her feel sick; all those months ago, he must have raped her again just before help had arrived.

Aveling had no idea how long she lay counting the stars in the night sky, but suddenly she became aware of someone touching her. Immediately she thought it must be Harry and that he had got to her again. But it was a group of rescuers, easing her onto a metal body frame, which was then pulled up to the top of the quarry.

Still confused, Aveling could hear many voices and sirens, then an elderly lady with white hair knelt beside her and gently stroked her head, murmuring, "It's ok, Aveling, we have got you. You're safe now."

She was vaguely aware of paramedics putting in needles, someone cutting her hands free, and a rubber mask was placed over her face. Then she passed out.

*

It was almost four weeks before Aveling regained consciousness, and that same old lady was sitting at the side of her bed. Immediately, she realised it was her English grandmother.

"Now, young lady, you gave us all quite a scare," she said kindly.

Aveling tried to sit up, but she was attached to various machines beeping around her bed.

Taking her granddaughter by the hand, Madam Aveling asked if she would like to know what had happened. She knew that the girl would be feeling a little disorientated.

"If things get too confusing, just tell me and I will stop," she assured Aveling. "But first you must know that Harry has been caught and is behind bars. So please do not even think about him for now.

"It has been four weeks since you were airlifted here. When you first arrived, your injuries were so severe that the doctors put you into an induced coma, so I will start by explaining all about your injuries first. Is that ok with you?"

When Aveling nodded, her grandmother continued. "You had fallen over forty feet and broke four ribs, your pelvis was fractured, you broke two bones in your legs and suffered a lot of bleeding. One of your hands had been crushed and needed a lot of surgery, and when you were taken into theatre, you had something called an ectopic pregnancy. So they had to remove one of your ovaries."

The older woman smiled kindly. "Do you remember who I am? I know it has been a long time since I last saw you."

"I think your face looks familiar," Aveling croaked. "Are you Grandma Aveling?"

"Yes, dear. Now I am afraid I have some more sad news for you. As you know, your Chinese grandma was selling up her estate, but she sadly passed away before she could leave there. Your father came to see you last week but had to return to London due to work. However, he is going to come and visit you when I get you home."

Madam Aveling knew this was a lot for her granddaughter to take in, but she felt the girl had to be told the truth from the start so that she could begin to process all the information.

Aveling was keen to know how she had been found, and asked if Harry had gone to get her help when she fell.

"No, dear. My driver James and I stayed at a local hotel in the village then kept watching the farmhouse, but it was so far back from the road that it was difficult to see anything. But when I worked with the police many years ago, they often said that the last person who saw the missing person is often the one who knows where they are.

"No-one visited his house all day, but I still believed he had something to do with you being kidnapped. So, when it turned dark, I sent James to knock on the front and back door, and if there was no answer to break into the property and check out the house.

"We knew the house had a cellar, and at first I thought he might have you locked up inside. But when we could not find him in the house, I had the feeling he must have another place close by where he could keep you indefinitely."

Aveling was intrigued as her grandmother went on, "James and I hid ourselves in the trees at the rear of the building and it was quite late when we saw him hastily coming from the direction of the old quarry. When he was out of sight, we headed over in that direction, hoping he would not see us.

"We checked out the old buildings there but found nothing. Just as we reached the last one, I saw a pair of panties screwed up in a corner. I just knew that's where he must have held you, because when I picked up the knickers, they were still wet."

The older lady paused for a moment before continuing. "At first I feared the worst, thinking he had murdered you, and I started to look around to see if there were any new mounds of earth. It was then my attention was drawn towards the quarry itself. At that point the police arrived, demanding to know who we were.

"I just prayed he hadn't pushed you over the top of the quarry, but when I stepped closer and closer to the edge, I thought I heard you calling me. With the torch, we eventually saw something halfway down the side of the quarry. I know now it was nine yards of silk fluttering in the wind like a huge banner. It must have got caught up on the ledge and drawn the light from the torch directly towards you.

"When the emergency services pulled you up, they told me you couldn't have called out for me because your injuries were too severe, so I don't know what I heard. And I don't know how the nine yards of silk was on that ledge with you, but I did send someone to retrieve it later, as I know it was a gift from your late grandma."

Madam Aveling's voice cracked with emotion. "I feel so guilty, Aveling. If only I had found you earlier. But I know now the police were suspicious of Harry's story, and they were watching and waiting for him to make a move, like me and James."

Aveling remained in hospital for another few weeks to recover from her injuries and was visited every day by her grandmother. When she was ready to go home, it was decided that she would go to stay with Madam Aveling rather than her father and his new family.

*

Aveling had never seen her grandmother's home and did not know what to expect. So, when the car pulled off the road then through huge iron gates into a sweeping driveway, her first view of the castle took her breath away. If Mary's family home had been grand, this was something else. It reminded her of being a little girl and seeing castles in fairytale books.

Madam Aveling had instructed all the men who worked at the castle to avoid young Aveling when possible, to keep out of her way, and never be alone with her in any room. The last thing she wanted was to see her granddaughter feel or be afraid.

It was only once she was settled at her grandmother's home that Madam Aveling told her how Dr Tommy had visited daily while she was in a coma. But he hadn't visited the hospital again once she woke up.

One evening, while chatting to the private nurse/bodyguard who had been engaged to cover the night shift, the woman had revealed that the doctor still popped in every night when Aveling was asleep.

"He told me he was your doctor and just needed to monitor your vitals. It didn't seem normal, but he's a doctor so I didn't question him any further."

When the story was relayed to her grandmother, she was concerned. Although he was Dr Valerie's grandson and had been the one who had called for help in the first place through the newspaper ad, Madam Aveling was unsure of his intentions towards her granddaughter. When she had collected Aveling on being discharged from hospital, she had provided a false set of details, as she was still wanted by the police.

The winter came and went, and Aveling slowly began to regain her physical strength. Her grandmother knew it was going to take a long time before the young girl would get her confidence back, but Madam Aveling had a few plans of her own.

As a young woman, she had known all about the evil in the world and how some things could fester for a lifetime. No matter how long it would take, she was determined to get revenge for Aveling, as she believed only then her granddaughter would be able to come to terms with what had happened.

While she intended to keep her granddaughter informed at every step, there were some details she believed Aveling would not be able to handle, so she would keep them to herself and a few close male friends who she knew would do anything for her.

She had often heard the phrase that people who look for revenge should first dig two graves. But she would always reply, "People who destroy the lives of others need to know there are people like me in the world, who are more than happy to get dirty and become gravediggers." Regardless of how many graves she would need to dig, she would have her revenge for her granddaughter.

Madam Aveling believed that, like playing a game of chess, the best moves needed careful planning. And as her granddaughter had not mentioned the rape again since she arrived at the castle, she needed to know if young Aveling still wanted to get revenge.

After a few moments of thought, the girl agreed that she did – not just for her, but for all the other girls those boys had harmed. As Harry was in prison, trying to get moved to a psychiatric by playing the crazy card, Madam Aveling decided they should begin with the person who started Aveling's nightmare – Mary.

The girl had continued to deny having anything to do with Aveling's kidnapping, and her statement to the police stressed that she had no idea Harry would do such a thing and that her family had not been involved. So, Madam Aveling suggested she should invite the girl over to visit them at the castle.

The conversation went well and Mary sounded excited about seeing her schoolfriend again. She did not know that Aveling had overheard her telephone conversation with her brother on the day she was attacked by Harry. So, she had no idea that her visit was part of the two Avelings' plan for revenge.

When the Rolls Royce, driven by James dressed up in his chauffeur's uniform, went to pick Mary up at the station, Aveling went along to see Mary's face. The girl had always been materialistic, but when she saw the castle her jaw almost hit the ground in disbelief. Aveling, playing it very cool, simply said, "Yes, this is the family home."

CHAPTER 9: REVENGE

Madam Aveling had just finished a meeting with a young man who she referred to as her little helper. Lee had been a very skinny boy when he first joined the staff at the castle, but now he was six feet tall with the muscles of a body builder. He had joined the farmhands on the estate when his lordship had still been alive and had quickly become one of the master's favourites. The duke had been keen to offer a boy who had experienced such a bad start in life the chance to enjoy guidance and a good stable family.

When the duke passed away, Madam Aveling offered Lee the chance to go to university or if he needed anything at all, but he wanted to stay at the estate, as he had promised he would take good care of Madam Aveling. Now in his late twenties, there was nothing the young man would not do for her.

Always kind and thoughtful, nevertheless Lee had a wicked temper. And while it was rare to witness, once he lost it everybody knew to keep out of his way. After working on the farm for so long, he had a physique that most men would envy, and while he was always popular with the local ladies, he never seemed interested in any of them.

Over the years the young man had become remarkably close to Madam Aveling; almost like another son. But he had earned himself the nickname 'Vanish' by the other staff, due to the fact that he seemed to quickly see off the many prospective suitors keen to capture Madam Aveling's heart.

Madam Aveling did have one remarkably close friend who was welcome at the castle, and Prince Antony, Lee, and the housekeeper/driver James, spent many evenings together playing cards and bridge. The prince and Lee also spent hours playing chess, as they were well matched. Madam Aveling did play, though not at their level, but she always seemed to be extremely lucky when it came to playing cards, particularly poker. Prince Antony suggested it was because she never had what was called a tell, which made her difficult to beat.

There was no doubt that if she ever had a problem on the estate, these three men would stop at nothing to make Madam Aveling happy and help her out. So when they were told about her granddaughter's attack and kidnap, they were quick to offer their assistance.

The prince had contacts all over the world, and Lee had the muscles. Once they received instructions in what Madam Aveling referred to as her game of human chess, they were ready to go into action.

When Mary and Aveling returned from the railway station, Lee was at the door to greet them. To Aveling's surprise, her grandmother introduced him as Baron Lee, and he was wearing a very expensive suit and a dazzling diamond that had once belonged to the duke.

Lee's first move was to make a big fuss over Mary, and she quickly began to act the same way as she had with Harry. It didn't take her long to tell the staff what she wanted, expecting them to climb two flights of stairs just to bring her a glass of water. Normally, Madam Aveling would not have allowed anyone to boss her staff about, as she had always treated them with kindness. But she had already reassured them that this was a one-off situation, and asked them to bite their tongues while Mary was there.

Within days, the girl was hooked. She was following Lee around the castle, calling him her little baron, and spending more time chasing after him than with Aveling.

Lee was surprised she had taken the bait so quickly, but he played his part well and talked about his family back in eastern Europe with a huge castle and large acres of land. He explained that he had only come across to England to look for a new car but had been invited to stay at the castle, as his family were good friends with Prince Antony's family back home. He said he was staying with Madam Aveling till his new car – a Bentley – was ready, as he had requested the seats should all be embroidered with his family crest.

Over the next few weeks Mary made many improper suggestions, only too keen to please him. Everything she said was reported back to Madam Aveling, but only a fraction of the conversations were relayed to her granddaughter. It seemed Mary was keen to stress that she liked to have fun, and even Madam Aveling and the prince had never heard of her bizarre suggestions. It was Lee who had to explain to them what a golden shower was.

Lee took Mary horse riding regularly and bought her several expensive gifts, but this started to niggle Aveling. Feeling left out, she couldn't see where or how the revenge her grandmother talked about would start.

When she finally asked her grandmother when things would change, Madam Aveling explained, "Don't worry. Things often look good just before a storm. I promise you this is all part of the plan."

"But, Grandma, what if Lee falls in love with her?"

"My dear child. I know Lee well enough to know he is just doing his job, and if for any reason I feel he is in over his head, I will move on to the next person who hurt you and come back to Mary later," Madam Aveling assured her. "People who did what they did to you are going to feel the full force of my revenge. But please remember, Aveling, this is not just for you. Think about all the other girls they have hurt and whose lives have been destroyed. Mary and her brothers will all be sorry by the time I have finished with them.

"One thing the old duke taught me was to have patience," he added. "Bad people always think they can get away with anything, but not with my family. I have everything under control."

That evening, over dinner, Madam was paying close attention to her granddaughter's facial expressions. Shortly after Mary began giggling and pretend feeding Lee, young Aveling asked to be excused due to a headache.

Later in the evening, Madam Aveling and Prince Antony were enjoying coffee in the sitting room when they suddenly heard an ear piercing sound coming from the great hall.

They rushed out to find Mary looking very sheepish on the mezzanine, with young Aveling lying on the floor in pain screaming. Lee had already reached the young girl, and he looked worried while Prince Antony – a former military doctor – gently checked her over. It was clear that she had a dislocated arm, so the prince didn't waste any time and quickly pulled the arm to relocate it into the shoulder.

Mary had left the mezzanine and joined the others on the lower floor as Madam Aveling asked, "What the hell happened?"

It was Lee who spoke first. "I have no idea," he replied. "One minute Aveling was on the ladder going up to the mezzanine, and when I turned around she was on the floor."

Mary quickly chipped in, "She was on the ladder, and it dislodged from the top rail, then Aveling fell backwards."

Madam Aveling didn't believe a word that came out of Mary's mouth, but she asked Lee to carry Aveling back to the living room, where she was given painkillers and a chance to rest and calm down.

Once she was settled, Lee asked Mary to take a walk in the gardens with him, but as they were leaving the room, he looked over his shoulder and gave Aveling a little smile.

Madam Aveling asked her granddaughter, "Are you ok? Can you tell me what happened, or did you just slip off the ladder?"

Before she could ask any more questions, Aveling scanned the room to see if they were alone, pausing to give the prince a look.

"It's ok, Aveling," her grandmother told her. "He knows everything, and you are safe to trust him."

The girl went on to explain that she had been going down the ladder, not up, when it started to move. And as she looked up to the mezzanine, she saw Mary pushing the ladder clear of the rail.

"I don't feel safe with her being at the castle any longer," she announced.

"That's ok," her grandmother reassured her. "I have already booked Mary's return ticket, and she will be leaving in the morning. If you are still worried at bedtime tonight, you can sleep in my room until she has gone."

*

The following morning, Lee dropped Mary off at the station and hurried back to the castle to fill Madam Aveling and the others in on everything the girl had said that week. He was still blaming himself for not being able to help Aveling the previous night and was convinced if he had been quicker he could have broken her fall.

"Why did Mary want to hurt her?" Madam Aveling asked. "I can't understand it."

Lee replied, "I believe she is jealous of her, and it was probably made worse when she asked me what Aveling meant to me, and I said she was very special to me." He looked embarrassed.

"It was just something that slipped out, I'm afraid, but I believe she wanted Aveling out of the picture."

He went on to tell the others how Mary had clung to him at the railway station and pleaded with him to come and visit her as soon as possible, as her parents and brothers would love him. "She even suggested that I should take Aveling with me."

On hearing this Aveling's face paled and she stared anxiously at her grandmother.

"Don't worry, my pet, you will never be going anywhere near Mary's brothers," Madam Aveling said calmly. "I think you are strong enough now to cope with the details of my plan. The first phase was to make Mary fall for Lee, and clearly she is besotted with him. Phase two, he will keep in touch through phone calls and emails and continue to stay close to her. But then Lee will explain he cannot spend any more time away from his home back in Europe, so he will propose marriage and pay a quick visit to Mary's home to pop the question and to formally ask her father for his blessing. As a member of a royal family, it would be the correct thing to do."

Sensing her granddaughter's confusion at the plans, Madam Aveling went on, "As you were raised in China, I don't know how much you know about weddings here in England, but normally the bride's parents pay for the wedding. Knowing Mary, she will want the best of everything, so if I were her parents I would do a background check on Lee. Prince Antony and his family have put together one hell of a package, so it would take an army of detectives to get past that red tape." She couldn't hide her smirk.

"Mary will be told by Lee that he wants her to wear his mother's diamond ring, but in reality we are going to acquire an estate ring with all the necessary paperwork – one I know a girl like Mary would never reject. On one of the nights when Mary has been drinking heavily – as she often does – Lee will get her to sign what she will be told is an insurance document. But in fact it will be a receipt of purchase in Mary's name only, with the balance due one week after the wedding, for £250,000."

Aveling shook her head, still looking confused. "Do you mean Lee is actually going to marry Mary?"

Her grandmother laughed. "Silly Billy, I have no intention of allowing a girl like that to marry Lee or to join my family, but for now we need to make sure Mary believes it is for real. And when a father has only one daughter, he will want only the best for her."

"But, Grandma, what will happen to Lee if he cancels the wedding? Won't her brothers come after him?"

"No, because just a few hours before the wedding, we have set up a trap. So for now, Aveling, you have to trust us."

"What will we do if Mary sends us an invitation?" Aveling persisted.

"I've thought about that," assured her grandmother. "Your father has asked me to go over to China to sort out your grandmother's estate, and I will need you to come along and translate for me. I have already set up someone to run the estate till we get there, so there is no rush. As for the wedding, Prince Antony will be there to back Lee up. I promise you, everything is going to be ok."

*

Over the next few weeks Lee would call or email Mary almost every night, sending her little gifts and flowers – under Madam Aveling's direction – to keep her hooked. And each time she asked him to visit, his reply was always the same, "Sorry, Mary, you know I have to work from here for now. But don't worry, it's not long until the wedding."

One evening Madam Aveling caught her granddaughter listening into Lee's conversation outside the door. Later she asked her directly what was wrong, but Aveling just shrugged her shoulders and walked away.

Madam Aveling knew that girls who had experienced the kind of trauma that her granddaughter had would often turn their fears inside out, trying to make sense of their lives. She also knew that some could never come to terms with being raped. As young Aveling had already tried to kill herself once, her grandmother was keen to keep a close eye on her and be there for her if the girl crumbled.

*

It was the Thursday before the wedding, but Madam knew that all the payback was about to happen on the Glenhall estate, so it was time for her and her granddaughter to leave for China. Madam Aveling knew she had to keep her granddaughter's mind occupied.

Early that morning Lee and the prince had left to travel to Mary's family estate. That Friday would be the men's stag do, so Lee was driving a new two-seater sports car that Mary had asked him for as a wedding gift. The car was only on loan, so for him it was just another prop.

The week before the wedding Madam Aveling had received a phone call from an old acquaintance saying she had been at the hairdressers and overheard Mrs Glenhall saying how much Mary's family were looking forward to the wedding and that Mary's new husband had a title and a rich family. The woman had been boasting how much the wedding was costing, but saying that nothing was too much for her daughter, who would become a baroness after the wedding.

Madam believed all was set to go at the Glenhall estate, and she knew she would not hear from Lee again till the Monday after the chaos.

CHAPTER 10: THE LONG JOURNEY

On the plane to China, Aveling seemed to be miles away, deep in thought, until eventually her grandmother asked her if everything was ok.

"It's Lee, Grandma. What if something goes wrong?" she asked, her face a picture of concern. "I think it was a mistake to leave him."

"Lee can take care of himself," her grandmother replied emphatically. "Now, I know I asked before we left, but I just want to check you remembered to bring the nine yards of silk and three pieces of jade from your late grandma?"

"Yes, but why do we need to take them with us?" Aveling frowned, then looked closely at her grandmother. "And how did you know about the silk and jade?"

Madam Aveling smiled. "Ever since your mother and father married, I have been in contact with your late grandma and grandad, through the diplomatic bag. It wasn't easy because of the language difficulties, but when I came to see you as a baby in China, I made time to see your grandma. As you know, you are the only grandchild for both families, so very precious to us all.

"Just before your late grandma passed away, she sent me a letter which I've had translated. Would you like to read it?"

When Aveling nodded, her grandmother reached into her bag and brought out an envelope.

Aveling read, "*My dear friend, if you are reading this, I will no longer be there for Aveling, so please take care of her for me. I know you will remember our conversation about the silk and jade, so I do not want to put the details in writing. When you come over to settle my estate, please make sure she has those two things with her. Give her my love, and when the deed is finished, take care of it for me.*"

Aveling finished reading and turned to her grandmother. "What did Grandma mean when she said 'it'?"

"I cannot say any more right now, but I promised your grandma when it's time you will see for yourself."

*

Back in England, Lee was getting ready for the stag night. Not long after they arrived at the venue, Mary's brother Sam introduced one of the other guys as Harry. Lee immediately looked at the prince and frowned.

After the party, the prince asked Mary's brother Mark if the Harry at the party was Mary's ex and was a little shocked to hear it was. Mark did add that the relationship was over now.

When Prince Antony relayed the information back to Lee later that evening, the two men realised Harry must have been released on bail.

"Well, I wasn't expecting that," huffed the prince.

"Neither was I. Do you think we have any problem with our existing plan?" Lee asked.

The other man shook his head. "Not for now, but let's just keep going with the plan we have and we will take care of Harry later."

Antony had asked his younger brother Pip to travel over from Europe to be Lee's best man, and when he was filled in on the details of their plan, he was only too happy to help. It was agreed that Pip would fly in by private helicopter a few days before the wedding, and stay with Mary's family.

As he was also a prince, Mary's family were extremely happy to say yes. Pip, who had been born to the king and his second wife, was over twenty years younger than his brother, and he was one of those men who had everything – title, money, estates, love of travel. To top it all off, he was extremely handsome.

Antony had explained the story of Aveling's kidnap and also revealed that Mary had set the poor girl up to be raped by her brothers. In the prince's world, sex with a girl, any girl, had to be consensual. The story of how Harry kidnapped Aveling from the hospital, where she should have been safe, seemed bizarre. But learning the details of how Harry had treated Aveling made Pip extremely angry.

First, though, it was Mary's turn to receive her punishment. It was Pip's job to do his best to get Mary into bed, and he had brought along a friend to video everything, on the pretext that he was covering the wedding.

Pip thought it might take him a few days to get Mary into bed, but the day he arrived she was there to greet him. As she showed him around the grounds and estate, he could not believe his luck when she led him into an old barn and immediately moved in for a kiss. Pip was only too happy to oblige, and when she started to undress him, he was just hoping his friend was filming. As she slipped her own clothes off, he turned slightly and spotted the camera in a gap in the barn wall so knew his friend was nearby.

When they were both naked, the prince began to ravish her like a dog with a bone. Mary, surprised, asked him not to be so rough, but he ignored her and became rougher until she was begging him to stop. When he had finished, she started to protest, but he was quick to remind her she had been the one who had started things.

Later that day, he caught up with his friend recording views to add into the wedding video later. The cameraman revealed that he had caught Mary and one of her brothers talking on film. When he replayed the conversation, Mary could clearly be heard plotting how she could get the prince having sex with her on tape, as she intended to use it to blackmail him later. To Pip, this was dynamite, and he was looking forward to playing along.

The next morning he was just getting dressed when Mary came into his bedroom, still in her nightdress. Pip saw her cunningly press a switch on a hidden camara on the dresser top, but he pretended not to see. Little did she know he had his own hidden camera already recording.

As their first encounter had been rough, he was a little surprised she wanted more, but this time he decided to be gentle. Her silk nightie slipped off like butter on a hot knife as he pushed her gently onto the bed, and he struggled to restrain himself as he entered her.

For a man like Pip, used to getting his own way, being gentle was not easy but somehow he managed.

When she got up from the bed, he noticed her surreptitiously going to the dresser to switch the camera off, so he knew he could now pull her back for round two – unrecorded. This time, though, he would take her just as he wanted. Mary started to put up a fight which only turned him on more, and as he pushed her back down on the bed again, it was clear she thought she knew what was coming.

But she was so very, very wrong. Suddenly he flipped her over to take her from behind, and when she tried to scream, he held his hand over her mouth to muffle the sound. It was clear she had never been taken that way before, and as he forced his penis hard inside her anus, she struggled against him. When he had finished, he stood up and dragged her to her feet, then told her to get the fuck out of his room.

Shaking with emotion, Mary told him she would tell her brothers. But Pip had already expected that.

He grabbed her by the neck and said quietly, "One word out of you, and you can cancel the wedding on Saturday and say goodbye to all the money your parents have already spent."

*

Lee had arranged to meet Pip and his brother Antony before the wedding, but the weather was bad, so they didn't get a chance to meet in advance. As the bride walked down the aisle with all eyes on her, Lee could only hope that their plan would go without a hitch.

The original plan had been for Pip to stand up to object when asked if anyone had any objections to the wedding. He would then announce that he'd had sex with the bride, so in his opinion Mary was not good enough for his friend. Then they would all just storm out of the church.

But Pip had another plan. He arranged a huge screen in front of the congregation so that the people at the back of the church could see as the bride walked down the aisle. The church was filled with family, friends, and estate workers, and it was standing room only. When the screen filled with this stunning image of the bride and her father walking towards the altar, the ladies in the congregation drooled at the sight. Her dress was beautiful, the long train spreading out behind her, and the tiara on her head looked like a family antique, covered in what looked like diamonds that sparkled in the church lights.

Pip nodded towards his cameraman friend, and the screen showed Mary walking happily down the aisle towards the groom before it suddenly cut to the clip of Mary planning to blackmail the prince. It then went directly onto the recording of Pip getting dressed in his bedroom when Mary entered wearing only a nightie.

The congregation sat in silence as the screen showed two naked people having sex, and the poor vicar didn't know what to do or what to say. Halfway down the aisle, Mary screamed for someone to stop it, but no-one moved, not even her father.

Suddenly her brother Mark jumped into action and tried to knock over the screen, but the damage was already done.

Lee walked calmly towards Mary's father and paused just long enough to announce that the wedding was off. Then he stormed out of the church with the two princes following.

*

Lee's sports car had already been packed with his and Mary's belongings, as he had kept up the pretence that the couple would go directly off on honeymoon. But when he left the church with Antony, he drove straight to her house and dumped her bags on the doorstep, then headed down the long driveway to the exit gates.

Instead of making their way back to the castle, though, Lee had something else in mind and he turned in a different direction at the end of the driveway – towards Harry's farmhouse.

When they got there, Harry had just arrived back from the abandoned wedding. He was just about to put his key into the door lock when he saw Lee getting out of the car. He froze to the spot as Lee demanded to know why the hell he was not still in jail.

Without waiting for any reply, Lee stormed forward until he was face-to-face with Harry, then began punching him again and again, fury getting the better of him. Prince Antony was worried

Lee wouldn't know when to stop, so he climbed hastily out of the car and pulled his friend back.

Lee's anger took some calming, but Antony knew if he did not get Lee back into the car quickly, he would end up killing Harry. Leaving the young man lying at his front door in a bloody heap, they got back into the car and headed back to the main road.

As they passed near the church and could see many of the shocked guests leaving, they saw Pip's helicopter taking off from a nearby field. Within minutes, Antony's phone beeped with a text from his brother.

He laughed and read to Lee, *"Thank you for the best weekend I have had for a very long time. The show was just great, and the idea that someone thought she could blackmail me... well, that was the icing on the cake. Thank you, lads, and let me know if you ever need me again. PS, I have left a little gift for Aveling back at the castle."*

CHAPTER 11: THE FLIGHT

Lee and Antony, both sporting huge grins, had not been driving long when the phone rang. Prince Antony put the call on speaker and they heard Mary begging for another chance, saying how sorry she was, claiming everything had been blown up out of proportion and that Prince Pip had taken advantage of her.

After a few minutes of listening to her tearful voice babbling, Lee hung up without saying a word. With a frown, he glanced at his passenger.

"I thought that was mission completed," he said, "but we now know Harry is out on bail, so he still needs to pay."

When they returned to the castle, he sent a message to the hotel in Hong Kong where Madam Aveling and her granddaughter were staying. As her son was a diplomat, they knew that all her emails, letters, and phone calls would be monitored in and out by the Chinese government, so Lee kept his email short.

He and Prince Antony were scheduled to fly out and join the women in a few days, so it would be better to share the whole story then.

In the meantime, Madam Aveling was treating her granddaughter to several shopping trips in a bid to keep her mind off worrying about the prince and Lee. At one point she joked that if they bought much more she would need to hire a shipping container to take it all back to England.

*

Lee had never been on a plane before, so the excitement started a few days later as soon as they arrived at the airport. He was taken aback by how big the plane was, then extremely anxious about whether it would get to Hong Kong safely. When he asked the prince where the parachutes were kept, just for fun Antony joked they were under the seats with the life jackets.

When Madam Aveling and her granddaughter arrived at the airport to collect the two men, Prince Antony took great delight in teasing Lee that it had been like travelling with a big baby on the flight. The biggest surprise, though, was when Aveling rushed forward and threw her arms around Lee as though they had been apart for years.

Madam Aveling had told all her staff, including Lee, to stay away from Aveling when she first arrived at the castle, because she was worried that the girl was traumatised by men in general. And she thought it would take her granddaughter a long time to learn to trust or want to be involved with any man. Aveling's reaction to Lee's arrival now made Madam Aveling question whether she had been right to bring him to China.

To Lee, everything was so strange – the smells, the sights, the colours seemed so much brighter; the food even tasted so different.

When they all met up for a meal that evening at a local restaurant, Aveling was full of questions about what had happened at the wedding. She was told that everything had gone to plan, but she persisted in asking questions until her grandmother eventually gave in and explained what had happened with Prince Pip and the screen at the church.

"Mary and her family have been left with a huge bill for the wedding expenses, and she will be receiving a bill for the engagement ring very shortly," Madam Aveling said. "I promise Mary's reputation is well tainted, and it will take years for her family to recover financially. So, be a good girl and let's draw a line under the wedding that never was."

As Lee started to eat his meal, Aveling noticed his hands were covered in bruises, but before she could ask any more questions, Lee leant closer to her and said quietly, "You heard what your grandma said, no more questions."

The last thing the prince and Lee wanted was to explain to Madam why Harry was at large, so for now they would keep that detail to themselves.

As they ate their meal, Madam Aveling noticed a couple sitting nearby who seemed to be keeping a watch over them, so she was careful to keep the conversation very general, as she knew anything that got overheard would end up in the government's hands.

*

The following morning, the four set off to drive to Aveling's late grandparents' estate. Built many years before in the very old style, there were a number of buildings grouped together in a compound for family members, all sharing the same courtyard.

The paperwork just to get them into the estate was mind-blowing, so by the time they eventually arrived at the house they were exhausted and ate a quick snack prepared by the housekeeper, then retired for the night.

The next day after breakfast, Madam Aveling asked the housekeeper if he could fetch more supplies from the store. She did not really need anything, but she knew anything he overheard would be passed on to the local admin office.

She was ready to explain to the others exactly why they were there and why Aveling had been asked to bring the silk and jade, but first she checked around all the buildings looking for the best exits, should they be necessary.

Madam Aveling then sent her granddaughter to fetch the nine yards of silk and the three pieces of jade. As they all looked on bewildered, Madam Aveling ran the silk across the table and explained she was following the last instructions she had been given by Aveling's late grandma.

"She told me that if you lay out the silk, you will find a map. However, that conversation was years ago when the silk was in good condition, so it might be difficult since it has been blowing off a ledge in the quarry.

"She told me that it takes some finding, as the thread of silk is only a little different and was twisted and woven with the finest of gold, while the silk was cream. But apparently, if you very gently splash some water on it, the gold shows as a little darker in colour."

The others looked totally bewildered; they had no idea about the map in the silk.

Lee was first to speak. "Do you really mean we are here for a treasure hunt?"

Madam Aveling shrugged. "Well, that all depends on what you would call treasure," she replied. "But what I can tell you at this time is we need to progress slowly, we must only talk when we are sure no-one can overhear us, and never write anything down. So if anyone ask you any questions, please say nothing other than that we are here to settle up the estate." She adopted a more businesslike tone. "Let's just see if we can make any sense of this damaged silk."

"Grandma, what about the jade?" Aveling asked.

"For now, keep it with you at all times and don't stray too far from one of us," her grandmother stressed. "I will tell you more as we continue, but now let's get to grips with this silk map."

They all walked around the table studying the silk, but no-one could see any signs of a map no matter how long they looked. Madam Aveling was beginning to doubt if they had the right silk.

"Aveling," she asked, "when we retrieved the silk from the quarry, did you wash it?"

"No, Grandma," she replied.

After another half an hour of everyone studying and staring at the silk, Madam Aveling decided they should take a break and try again later.

Aveling offered to take Lee on a walk around the compound to show him where she had spent so much time with her grandparents, and he was only too happy to accept. Everything was so new to him. The gardens were immaculate, and he had never seen some of the flowers and trees with so much blossom.

As they were strolling companionably in the gardens, they were approached by a stranger. Lee was immediately suspicious, as the compound was surrounded by a huge wall with iron gates, and access was only possible with a key.

The stranger was coming out of some sort of garden structure, and as he reached them he asked what they were doing there. He looked directly at Lee when he spoke, but of course Lee didn't know a word of Chinese.

Aveling responded in a very strong tone of voice, although Lee did not understand what she said. "Never mind us," she told the man in Chinese. "I have all the necessary paperwork to this place, so why are you here on this property?"

The stranger looked stern and, without an answer, stormed off towards the exit gate.

When Aveling and Lee returned to the house, she told her grandmother about the man and said she'd seen him coming out of the old cave entrance. Lee looked bewildered as he hadn't seen any cave, but Aveling explained that the wooden structure at the entrance had been styled as a child's playhouse and built by her grandfather to cover the entrance to a cave. It had also been somewhere she could play when she came to stay with them.

Madam Aveling looked concerned. She knew her granddaughter would have been careful when she saw the stranger, but in China you even had to be careful with your tone of voice as much as with your words. She suggested they all went to see if anyone could get access to the cave.

The gardens around the compound stretched for over a mile, and at the rear of the property was a sheer cliff face which Aveling was never allowed to go near as a child.

Madam always liked to be prepared for anything, so before they set off she told Aveling to bring the silk map with them. As she was not as young or fit as the others, it took them a good thirty minutes to reach the structure. When they went through the doorway, it was beginning to show signs of decay but everything seemed to look normal.

Taking their time, the group explored all the other rooms, On entering what would have been an old bedroom, Aveling scanned the room and so many memories flooded into her mind all at once. Noticing the tears on her face, Lee put an arm around her shoulders to comfort her. Madam Aveling and the prince were surprised Aveling let anyone to touch her, but they were keen to know why she was upset.

"I just remembered something my grandfather told her, and it was always told to me like a poem. 'If you are afraid, just shine the light, from day to twilight throw the silk up high to see your way home, and you will never be alone.'" Aveling began to sob as she said the words.

"Ok," her grandmother decided, "it's getting late so let's call it a day and we will come back another day."

CHAPTER 12: TRUST NO-ONE

By the time they returned to the house, a group of men in uniforms and armed with guns were gathered in the courtyard, talking to the man who looked after the estate. One with the most decorations on his uniform stepped forward and asked who was responsible for the house.

Before anyone could answer, one of the other men stepped forward and pointed to Aveling. She was the only one who could understand the language, so she listened to his instruction then put her bag on the floor and pulled out a form giving her permission to be there. She offered it to him, then he demanded to see all the passports. Without explaining to the others, Aveling dashed inside and returned with all four passports.

When Madam saw what was in her hand, she began to feel a little anxious, but she knew not to show any signs of fear. The man took his time looking at each person then pairing them up with their passport pictures, and finally he wrote down the passport numbers before returning them to Aveling.

Without another word to the group, he then waved his hands, gave out some orders to his men, and they all turned and marched towards the exit. As they watched them leave, Aveling put her fingers to her lips to shush the others until the men had marched out of sight.

"What was all that about?" Lee asked eventually.

Aveling explained that the man she and Lee had encountered earlier had reported them to the local authorities, so the officers had come to check their reasons for being there.

Frowning, Aveling told them she wasn't convinced the questioning was just routine. "I struggled to answer some of the questions about my granddad, and it was only when I told the officer I was the only granddaughter of the late owners, who had been connected to the government in some way, that things seem to relax a little." Aveling went on. "I don't really want to spend a day longer here than necessary. I remember as a child overhearing stories about how people would be there one minute then the next day would just simply disappear, without a word to friends or family."

Prince Antony admitted he felt nervous about the encounter and agreed the quicker they could solve the clue about the map the better.

Looking thoughtful for a moment, Lee asked if anyone else had seen the marks on the ceiling in the old playhouse. "I wasn't sure about it at the time and was going to mention it when we got back, but the soldiers were here to greet us."

None of the others had noticed anything, so they decided to quickly head back there to see what Lee meant and whether it had any connection to the nine yards of silk.

*

Back at the playhouse, Lee showed them what he had noticed.

The prince stared at the ceiling for a few minutes then asked Lee and Aveling to hold the silk up to the ceiling. He explained that the marks could be part of a star constellation, and where the thread changed direction was a clue. But the only constellation it would match up to was Gemini. "That makes no sense," he said.

"Actually, it might," Aveling said suddenly. "The name of the young concubine who escaped hanging was Gemini. That's what my grandmother told me."

They now realised that what they were looking at wasn't a map of land; it was a map to a star sign.

Lee asked Aveling if she knew of any way through the back walls that would give them access to the cave behind.

Looking a little embarrassed, Aveling admitted that whenever she had been to stay with her grandparents, her grandfather would often take her with him to camp out at the playhouse. He had always sworn her to secrecy about things she must never mention to her grandmother, and he had shown her how to get access, and how to avoid the traps.

"Traps?" Lee echoed. "It sounds like something out of a movie, Aveling. Is it too dangerous to enter?"

She shook her head. "Not if you stay close to me, but you may be surprised when we get to the end of the cave."

Without saying any more, Aveling led them all to a small room at the back of the playhouse. She had never been sure why her Chinese grandfather called it her playhouse, as it was about four times the size of the playhouses children had in the United Kingdom and could have easily housed a family of four.

Hoping the mechanism would still work, she went over to the last stone on the floor and placed one foot on it, then the other foot on the very next stone. Stretching out her arms, she pushed two stones on the wall and immediately a rumbling noise began, then slowly the wall started to move sideways.

"Why didn't you tell us all about the way into the cave?" Lee asked.

"Sorry," she smiled sheepishly. "I know you will find it hard to believe, but when I last visited the playhouse, I must have been only seven or eight. And daft as it sounds now, I totally forgot about it. It wasn't till you asked that I suddenly remembered what Grandfather had shown me."

Her grandmother did not look impressed. "If there are traps in there, I am too old for that. So, you two go and see if you can find any more clues, while Antony and I will stay here and wait for you."

Aveling took Lee's arm and stepped into the cave with only their mobile phone torches for light. But with one foot in and one out, Lee paused.

"Aveling, what kind of traps are we looking for? Are you sure your grandad told you about all of them?"

The girl laughed. "Well, I was only about eight at that time, but stop being such a baby. Come on." She pulled him into the cave then began to march ahead, leading the way.

Calling on her to slow down, Lee was beginning to feel more nervous with every step. And when she disappeared around a bend and out of sight, he grew more anxious. He was even more worried when he shouted her name and she didn't answer.

As he rounded the bend, light seemed to shine in, and he saw her sitting on the end of the cave looking out. He approached slowly in case he gave her a fright and she slipped off the end of the stone lip.

Turning to look up at him, Aveling smiled and patted the rock beside her, inviting him to join her. As he did, he was stunned by the view ahead of them. The sun lit up all the fields spanning for miles, and beyond them the mountains rose out of the ground like huge heaps of snow, the tops just disappearing out of view and into the clouds.

"Have you ever seen anything more beautiful in your life?" she whispered.

As his eyes made contact with hers, he gently put his arm around her waist, desperate to make sure she didn't slip. At that moment he realised he would always be there to protect her, but his feelings swung from those of a protective big brother to someone in love.

After a few minutes drinking in the view, Aveling said, "It's time to go. Grandma will be getting worried."

Lee stood up, reluctant to leave such a special moment in his life, and they slowly made their way back to the cave entrance.

Before they reached the others, he asked her, "Did you see any clues?"

She smiled. "Only one, and I will tell you all about it when we get back to the others."

CHAPTER 13: WHAT'S REAL?

Madam Aveling and the prince were waiting patiently outside the playhouse.

"Well," Antony asked eagerly, "did you find any clues?"

"Yes, one. Just before the bend, scratched into the wall were the words 'jade is the key'."

On the way back to the house, Lee explained that it wasn't really a cave, and he waxed lyrical about the incredible view they had seen. One thought still niggled him and he turned to Aveling.

"Why did you go so fast when we entered the cave. I was terrified?" he asked.

"Silly. I turned off the traps just as soon as I entered the cave," she replied with a cheeky look on her face that defied any attempt to scold her. "Come on, slow coaches, I'm starving. It must be time for dinner."

After their meal they sat around the table trying to make sense of what they had discovered – but it wasn't much. A star consolation Gemini was the only clue that would fit into the bands of gold left in the silk cloth, and the words 'jade is the key'.

After lots of discussion but no real progress, they decided to call it a day and get some sleep. The compound was miles away from any town or village, so when the lights went out, it was normally pitch-black outside. That night, however, the compound and the rooms were bathed in the golden light of a full moon.

Finding it difficult to sleep with so much whirling around his head, Lee decided to take a stroll around the compound, but when he opened the front door, he found Aveling standing on the decking. Mindful of startling her, he quietly said her name. As she turned slowly, he had to smile as he saw that the nightie she was wearing was covered with pictures of bunny rabbits.

His emotions whirling, he reminded himself of Madam Aveling's instructions to keep some distance between himself and Aveling since the attack in England. So, he was relieved when she said she had been struggling to sleep but was tired now, then she said goodnight and headed back to her room.

Left alone on the decking, his mind was spinning. Were his feelings for Aveling those of a brother? He'd never had a sister, so how was he supposed to know how that would feel? He'd had lovers before, but none had ever made him feel this way. And at the back of his mind were Madam Aveling's instructions not to get close to her granddaughter.

*

Aveling returned to her room, her own mind whirling with questions. Did Lee really like her? Or was he just another man wanting to use then abuse her? For the past few months she had given Lee a wide berth most of the time, but each time they got close she felt there was an invisible magnet inside her drawing her towards him. She just wanted to be wrapped up in his arms, as it seemed like the safest place on earth. But when he spoke to her, it felt like he was only interested in her as a sister, nothing more. Totally confused about her own feelings and Lee's, she determined to keep her distance.

CHAPTER 14: THE NIGHT PROWLER

When Aveling had stayed with her Chinese grandparents as a child, she would play with a neighbour's young daughter who was the same age. Next morning she decided that day she wanted to see if Maylu still lived in the same house. After the encounter on the decking the previous night, she was also keen not to hang around the compound with Lee.

She hoped if Maylu still lived nearby, they could have some time together to catch up. So she took an old bike from the bike shed and headed off out of the compound, a wave of her hand acknowledging Madam Aveling's shouts not to be more than two hours as they needed to get ready to leave.

Cycling down the road, she realised that so much time had passed since her last visit that a lot of the surroundings had changed. Totally disorientated, Aveling realised she was going in the wrong direction, so she dismounted and had a good look around to try and get her bearings.

At that moment, she saw the man they had seen leaving the playhouse. This time, he was wearing the same uniform as the other officers who had questioned them at the compound.

As he approached and asked if he could help, Aveling explained who she was looking for. He shook his head and said he had never heard of the family.

Asking if she was alone, he suggested he could escort her down the hillside to his parents' home and she could ask them if they knew Maylu's family and where they now lived.

*

Back at the compound, Madam Aveling was not too happy to see her granddaughter cycle off down the driveway on her own, but she knew she couldn't keep the poor girl away from the world for the rest of her life.

As the morning rolled on and there was no sign of Aveling returning, her grandmother grew more anxious and sought out Lee and the prince who were chatting on the decking.

When she expressed her fears, Lee asked if Madam Aveling had the address for Maylu.

She shook her head. "No I don't. All I know is Aveling said she was an old friend who used to live about a mile down the road. I saw Aveling checking out old bikes in the shed, then the last time I saw her she was cycling down the drive." Her voice broke slightly. "I told her not to be more than two hours… but that was three hours ago."

Her words struck fear in Lee's heart. Feeling uncomfortable about his feelings the night before, he had been trying to keep out of Aveling's way, but now it felt like someone was twisting a knife in his chest.

Rushing to the shed, he returned with an old bicycle, pausing briefly to ask Madam Aveling one question. "Did she turn left or right out of the gate?"

Madam Aveling hesitated then replied, "I'm sure she went right." Then Lee took off like a bat out of hell.

He didn't speak the language and he had no idea where to find her, but he believed the longer she was missing the more danger she would be in. Meanwhile the prince and Madam Aveling took the car and headed in the opposite direction.

Lee didn't want to miss any buildings, but the area was so barren that there was little to check. After almost an hour, he began to doubt if he was going in the correct direction, and he was growing increasingly worried for Aveling's safety. She didn't seem to understand how beautiful she was, with her green eyes and jet-black hair. He was scared if she had been taken by human traffickers, they would never see her again.

His mind in overdrive and his heart thumping hard in his chest, he began to scan the fields around him. There was an old building at the bottom of a dirt track and something was telling him that was the right way to go. But if he couldn't find her, how would he ever face her grandmother again?

As he reached the building, he heard a muffled scream and immediately jumped off the bike and ran as fast as his legs would carry him. The old door to the building was locked but one hard kick and it flew open. Inside, Aveling was fighting as a man held her, and immediately red mist took over Lee's thoughts. He pulled the man off then began raining punches on the man, blow after blow, only stopping when Aveling begged him to take her home.

He pushed the offender, bleeding, to the ground then hugged a shaking and sobbing Aveling and led her quickly out of the building. He knew his mobile phone wasn't working, so he asked if she could still ride the bike back, and he would be right there beside her all the way.

Each turn of the wheel seemed to go on forever and it felt like the longest journey of his life; only thinking how she must be feeling was driving him on.

When they returned to the house, Madam Aveling was waiting anxiously on the decking, and her heart jumped when she realised her granddaughter was with Lee.

Desperately hoping the girl had not been assaulted in any way, she decided not to ask questions until Aveling was ready to talk. Instead, she threw her arms around her and held her tight.

"It's ok, Grandma. Lee saved me. Nothing happened."

Lee briefly explained what had happened and the fight that had taken place, and they all agreed Aveling had been fortunate he had arrived in time.

Madam Aveling took command. "Right, go and get packed. We need to get the hell out of here now," she instructed. "And make sure nothing is left behind."

After everything was packed, Madam Aveling checked that they all had their passports then they got into the car ready to leave. At that moment, she saw a trail of lights in the distance, heading in their direction.

She told the prince, who was driving, not to switch on the headlights even though it was dark. It wasn't going to be easy, but she reckoned they would be able to see their way using the little moonlight available. He looked confused, but she said she would explain later.

When they reached the crossing checkpoint two hours later, she told him not to drive to the hotel, but to go directly to the British Embassy .

When they arrived, Madam held out their passports to the gate guards. He studied them carefully then asked if they had an appointment. At that point, Madam produced what looked like a credit card, which the guard put into a card reader at the security window.

He returned the card to her with a searching look, then the barrier lifted, and they drove into the Embassy grounds. Intrigued, Lee looked back and saw that the guard had immediately picked up the phone.

Like something straight out of a James Bond movie, their car was directed to a parking bay, and two men immediately approached with what looked like long poles with mirrors and began to scan the underside of the car.

Lee's hand stretched to the car door handle, but Madam Aveling quickly stopped him. "Don't worry, this is for our own safety," she explained. "Just wait until they tell us we can get out."

It took another ten minutes or so for a guard to open the door, then they were escorted out of the car and told to leave all luggage behind.

When they were escorted to the front door, Madam Aveling was greeted by a smartly dressed man who wrapped his arms around her and kissed her on both cheeks. Everyone looked on in disbelief, as Madam Aveling never got that close to anyone.

They were shown into a room and provided with food and drinks, then shown to a private floor, with bedrooms for all of them and a large living room . Their luggage had already been delivered and unpacked, although the suitcases themselves were missing.

Madam Aveling's briefcase was not there either. Although it was fairly tatty, it had once belonged to the old duke, and Madam always used it when travelling. As the prince knew their passports were in the briefcase, he couldn't hide his concern and asked her what was going on.

Madam Aveling put her finger to her lips and shushed them all, then began making small talk. But Lee wanted to know where their cases were.

"Everyone is tired," she replied with a warning frown. "It's better that we talk in the morning, but don't worry about the cases, they will be returned later. If you need anything during the night, don't go wandering around the Embassy. Just pick up the phone, and someone will bring whatever you need."

Once they had all headed off to their rooms for some sleep, Madam Aveling took a neatly folded handkerchief from her pocket then quietly left the room. Waiting for her outside the door was the same man who had greeted her in the lobby – Ambassador Brown.

Without speaking, they walked down a long corridor where a mirror was hanging on the wall, as though it was a dead end. But the Ambassador raised his hand to insert a keycard to the side of the mirror's frame, and it opened as if it was a door. Inside were two flights of stairs leading to a secure room.

One wall of the room was covered in screens, and Madam could clearly see the cameras covering her family's suite. As she had been instructed by one of the Embassy guards to leave the main light on in the living room on overnight, she and the Ambassador could clearly see one of the office girls enter the room.

The girl, who had just started working in the translation department a few weeks prior, began snooping around, examining every item – even opening up Madam Aveling's makeup compact.

She had witnessed many things in her lifetime, but Madam Aveling had to chuckle at how this was so blatantly a case of bad spying.

Grinning, the Ambassador told her, "This must be her first job. I guess some girls are just not born to be spies, but why would she believe she was going to get away with anything interesting?"

Madam pulled out the handkerchief which she had been given at the airport just before leaving England. "I guess she must be looking for this," she told him.

A series of numbers on the handkerchief blended in well with the pattern so would mean nothing to anyone except Ambassador Brown. But as Madam Aveling handed it over, she knew better than to ask him any questions.

Most of the staff did not have access to the top floor, which required an extra set of keycards just to get through the door. So the guards watching the screen were surprised that the girl, who had come over from Britain to take up the job a few weeks before and had passed all the stringent security checks, had got in and was moving quietly from one room to another.

But when she entered Lee's room, he must have been only half asleep and immediately switched on the bedside table lamp. Immediately, the snoop panicked and dashed out, not stopping until she reached the staff kitchen, where security guards were waiting to arrest her, watched on camera by Madam Aveling and Ambassador Brown.

Lee, stunned that there could be an intruder in the Embassy, dashed across the floor and crashed into young Aveling's room to see if she was alright. But when she woke to see the shadow of a man standing in only his boxer shorts, she didn't realise it was Lee at first and screamed so loud she could have woken the terracotta warriors.

To Madam Aveling and the Ambassador watching, it was like a scene from a Carry On movie, and they had to laugh at what they were watching.

The Ambassador's smiles faded when he received a message from one of the guards interrogating their spy downstairs. He was told she claimed she was only looking for small items she could sell quickly, as she needed the money.

Her story, he decided, would have sounded plausible anywhere else but not in the British Embassy. So, he ordered that she should be taken to a prison cell in the building to await further questioning.

CHAPTER 15: THE EMBASSY

Madam Aveling returned to the main room where everyone was now awake, and she quickly calmed them down with the explanation that the girl had been a thief looking for goods to sell. But the following morning, she and the Ambassador decided it would be best to explain the truth.

As they all sat down to eat breakfast, Madam Aveling took a large intake of breath and explained that her late husband had advised her if she was ever in trouble in China, all she needed to do was to get to the British Embassy.

"When my son began working here many years ago, I often travelled over to see him and spent time at many dinner parties when I visited. During that time, I became close friends with Ambassador Brown.

"When my son met and married a Chinese girl – Aveling's mother – naturally the Embassy had to run all sorts of checks on her background. Ambassador Brown had been a little concerned about me leaving Hong Kong to visit my son's new in-laws, and he had advised that if I was ever stuck for help in China I should contact him as soon as possible and he would organise help.

"The Ambassador also kindly set up a code between us, which I should use when contacting him. When we were leaving the compound yesterday, I sent the code from my mobile phone, so the Embassy was expecting us when we arrived."

Lee spoke first. "How did this intruder know anything about the nine yards of silk and three pieces of jade?"

But Madam Aveling explained that they believed the girl was not looking for specific items, just some expensive things that she could sell for extra money.

She went on to admit that she had been carrying a message for Ambassador Brown from England, and he was the only person she could give it to.

"Oh, Grandma, you mean you're a spy?" Aveling looked impressed.

Her grandmother shook her head. "No, I just carried the message. No spying involved."

Before they could ask any more, Madam Aveling received a call from the Ambassador to join him downstairs where the young intruder was being held.

As they entered the cell, it was clear the girl had been treated badly, as her face was covered in bruises. Madam Aveling looked furious but said nothing as the Ambassador gestured to her to sit down, then he asked his guards if they had extracted any further information from the prisoner.

"Yes, sir. She had been placed here for the long term as a sleeper and told she must lie low until required," one of the interrogators explained. "She had no idea she would have to be called to take action so soon."

Madam Aveling shook her head in disappointment, no longer angry. "I never expected that," she admitted. "I was so wrong. I don't like giving people the benefit of the doubt only to be let down so badly." She couldn't help but be saddened at how out of her depth the young girl looked.

When they left the holding cell, Madam Aveling and the Ambassador rejoined her family upstairs and offered them the chance to ask any more questions.

Ambassador Brown explained that he still did not believe the incident had anything to do with Aveling's nine yards of silk and three pieces of jade, but he said there had been a story which had circulated in China for many years about a huge treasure.

He told them it was like the story of King Arthur and the Knights of the Round Table, and how people believed there was a mythical sword out there, just waiting to be found and which would lead to a huge treasure and power.

In the case of China, the story many believed involved a young concubine fleeing from death, taking with her the secret of huge and priceless treasure which would need a convoy of lorries to take away. Other people simply wanted to retrieve the nine yards of silk and three pieces of jade as this was part of Chinese history, so they believed it would be priceless.

"But, Grandma, I thought you said earlier that the girl didn't want my silk and jade." Aveling looked confused.

Her grandmother shrugged. "Well, after talking with the Ambassador, we now think she could have been looking for two things. The first I believe she wanted was the message I was carrying. But I guess she could also have been looking for the nine yards of silk and three pieces of jade." Madam Aveling paused. "During her talks with the security team, the girl has still been holding back information, so for now let's just assume she wanted both."

Neither Ambassador Brown nor Madam Aveling mentioned the handkerchief she had given him the night before, and both were keen to wrap up any more questions.

The prince wanted to know what would happen to the young thief now, but the Ambassador informed him politely that any information in the Embassy was on a need-to-know basis, so they did not need to know what course of action would be taken.

He said he believed that the group had sparked the interest of the Chinese authorities when they arrived in the country, and from then on Aveling's late Chinese grandmother's home had been put under observation.

"From what Madam Aveling has told me, I think that they did not know about the treasure hunt, but the man you bumped into leaving the playhouse must have seen the silk folded neatly over your arm and decided he needed to investigate. It's possible when you all went into the playhouse, he saw the silk being lifted up to the ceiling to show the bends in the silk threads." Ambassador Brown paused briefly when he saw their shocked faces. "As he kept watching, he probably saw Aveling opening the cave entrance and he knew he was onto something good – possibly leading to a promotion with an increase in his wages.

"When he saw Aveline cycling down the hill alone, he intended to get her to show him how to disarm the traps inside the cave. But once they were in the old building, he decided he wanted to have sex with her and became very angry and aggressive when she fought him off.

"Thankfully, Lee turned up and fought the man off, then they left him injured on the ground. Obviously, Madam Aveline realised that the man would report them for the attack and the authorities would undoubtedly take the man's side.'

Madam Aveling interjected. "Although I have never seen the inside of a Chinese prison myself, I was warned years ago that many people went in but not all of them ever returned home."

Madam Aveling went on, "I knew we had to hurry, so when I saw vehicle headlights moving down the mountain that evening as we started to leave, I knew they were coming for us and I had to get everybody safely out of the country. I didn't want to frighten you all, but that's why I asked the prince not to use the car headlights as we left the commune."

As they were talking, they could hear loud noises coming from outside the Embassy, and when they moved to the window to investigate, they saw a large group of people all chanting, "Give us our treasure back!"

Ambassador Brown turned to Madam Aveling with a frown. "Did you find something you haven't told me about?" he asked.

"No, nothing." She shook her head. "We only have the silk and jade. As far as the silk is concerned, I always believed the real concubine's silk must have perished decades ago." She shrugged. "As for the jade, I have no idea why her late grandmother would tell her such a crazy story. It seems just like an old broken bangle. I was as surprised as everyone else when the Chinese agent broke into our room last night," she went on. "It feels as though this is all getting out of hand, so can you help us to get the hell out of here?"

The Ambassador frowned. "That's not going to be easy," he warned her. "I think we need to invite the Chinese Ambassador over here so that we can explain the situation. If we can't convince him, they will only send an agent to follow you all the way back to England. I don't think they will stop until they have the jade and silk."

That evening, following an invitation from Ambassador Brown, his Chinese counterpart turned up a little late, and they all gathered in the staff meeting room – everyone apart from young Aveling.

Madam Aveling began by explaining to their visitor when and where her granddaughter had been attacked, who the attacker had been, and why Lee and Aveling had returned from the farmhouse so quickly. Throughout the long story, the Chinese Ambassador sat and listened without betraying any emotion.

When she had finished, he stood up and announced that would like to meet up again in two days' time, when he would need to see Aveling. He also asked if he could see the items in question at that time and assured Ambassador Brown that the police would disperse the protesters outside.

When he left, Madam Aveling voiced her concern about how the authorities had found out about the nine yards of silk and three pieces of jade, particularly when she and the whole family had been so careful not to talk about them. *Could it all have been down to the man lurking around the old playhouse spotting the silk over Aveling's arm then being held up to the ceiling?* she wondered. *Had he really put the connection to the old story?*

*

Two days later, they met again with the Chinese Ambassador, but as they all settled around the table sipping tea, he asked if they could hold off on any questions as he was waiting for someone else to join them.

When the door finally opened, Aveling gasped as she saw the man who had attacked her in the farmhouse, and she recoiled as tears welled up in her eyes.

The Chinese Ambassador watched her face closely as he asked the army officer, now standing tall in his well pressed uniform with ribbons, what had happened when he saw Aveling that day. The man had not been informed why he was attending the meeting, but the colour drained from his face as the questioning began.

Pulling himself together, he tried to give a smart answer to every question. He explained they had received information on Madam Aveling's party and described what he had seen in the old playhouse with the silk.

At that point, Aveling was asked to produce the silk, which the Chinese Ambassador examined, looking decidedly unimpressed.

When he was shown the jade, he began to laugh and said he had seen nothing that would warrant any action from his office.

The Ambassador informed Madam Aveling that he was satisfied with what he had seen and that they were welcome to return to the compound belonging to Aveling's Chinese grandmother. But Madam said she had concluded her business, and they simply wanted to return home to Britain.

As everyone stood to leave, thinking the meeting was over, the Chinese Ambassador suddenly announced, "We have not yet concluded this meeting. There is one more thing I need to deal with." He turned to Aveling and asked her if she could tell him what had happened on the day she had been attacked.

With Lee squeezing her hand tightly to reassure her, she slowly gave her account of that day. On two occasions her attacker started to interrupt, but he was quickly and abruptly told to be quiet. Although only a few of the people in the room could understand Chinese, it was clear from the way the Ambassador spoke that he was firmly in charge.

When she had finished, the Ambassador asked if she could remember any marks on the attacker's body.

"Yes," she said with a slight shudder. "When he removed his trousers, I saw a large scar that looked like it had been caused by boiling water."

The room fell silent.

The Chinese Ambassador turned to the man and ordered him to remove his trousers. With a look of panic on his face, the man tried to stall by asking if he could go into another room with two of his officers who had travelled with him that day, to check for a scar. But the Ambassador repeated the order.

When he refused again, the Ambassador called the two officers who had travelled with the man to come in. As they did so, the air in the room was filled with tension. Even though Madam Aveling, the prince and Lee could not understand Chinese, it was clear the Chinese Ambassador was looking for something important.

The two soldiers were clearly uncomfortable about forcing their colleague to remove his trousers, but both knew that refusing would have huge consequences. As they followed the Ambassador's instructions, there was an audible gasp in the room as everyone in the room could see a scar clearly visible on the man's outer thigh.

The Chinese Ambassador stood up, ordered two of his own guards to escort Aveling's attacker outside, then bowed his head to everyone in the room and left.

As Aveling was still distraught at having to relive the attack, Lee put an arm gently around her shoulder to escort her out into the foyer.

As they entered the lobby ahead of Madam Aveling, the prince, and Ambassador Brown, the attacker and his two colleagues were being ordered by Embassy guards to collect their belongings from the holding office before leaving the building.

However, the Embassy staff didn't realise that the men had checked in handguns on arrival. So they were taken aback when the attacker suddenly picked up his gun, turned to where Aveling was still standing in the lobby, then pulled the trigger.

CHAPTER 16: THE GUN

Lee had seen the gun being lifted, and he quickly swung Aveling round to protect her with his body, while the gunman fired off another two shots before the Embassy guards pounced on him.

"Are you ok?" Lee asked Aveling. But as he did so, he slid down to the floor still holding onto her. He had taken two shots in his back.

And as Aveling answered, "Yes, I am fine," she hit the floor and realised she had also been wounded.

In the blink of an eye, the whole room seemed to go into organised panic. Madam Aveling had heard the shots but hadn't realised Lee and her granddaughter had been injured until she turned and saw their two bodies crumpled on the ground surrounded by Embassy staff.

Prince Antony and Ambassador Brown dropped to the floor and began applying pressure to the wounds while they waited for an ambulance to arrive.

Madam Aveling's whole world seemed to go into slow motion, but somehow she pushed herself forward into the first ambulance that arrived, demanding to travel to the hospital with her granddaughter. Lee was still being worked on when they left.

Later that day, after six hours of surgery, the doctor told Madam Aveling her granddaughter was still in a critical condition but should pull through. Relieved, her thoughts turned to Lee. But when she asked about his condition, the doctor assured her he would let her know, but for now it was not looking too good.

No-one could tell her where Prince Antony was, so she sat alone in the waiting room for another hour, her mind in turmoil, before she was allowed in to see Aveling who was still unconscious.

It was another three hours before the prince finally arrived, looking drained.

"Where have you been?" Madam Aveling asked him anxiously. "Where is Lee? How is he?"

As she fired questions at him, the prince dropped his head into his hands before replying that Lee's condition was touch and go, and he was in a bad way.

Lee had been like a son to her, and the news that she might lose him was almost more than she could take. The prince wrapped his arms around her as she sobbed, demanding to know where he had been when she'd needed him the most.

Once she was a little calmer, he explained. "I know you needed me, but Lee needed me more. I had to remove one of the bullets on the Embassy floor before we could move him. If I hadn't, he would never have made it." He paused briefly then went on, "He's not out of danger, but if he can just get through the next seventy-two hours, he will stand a chance."

The prince knew he would never convince Madam Aveling to return to the Embassy for some rest, so he booked a hotel room near the hospital so that she could close to hand if Lee or her granddaughter needed her.

It was about three in the morning when he finally convinced her to leave, and once he saw her settled in the hotel, he returned to the hospital. Lee was very dear to him, too.

Exhausted after the day from hell, the prince fell asleep in the chair beside the young man, and only woke when he heard the clatter of hospital trollies moving up and down. One of the nurses was checking on Lee's drip and monitor, and he asked if she could stay with her patient until he had a quick freshen up and checked on Aveling.

By the time he reached the girl's room, her grandmother was already at her bedside. As they talked quietly between themselves, Aveling began to come round.

"Where is Lee?" she croaked. "Is he ok?"

The prince was quick to assure her that Lee was doing ok in another part of the hospital, but the girl became extremely agitated.

"I want to see him, and I want to see him now," she said.

The prince looked at her grandmother and back to Aveling, then he told her she could see Lee just as soon as she could be moved. But for now, she needed to stay put.

"Ok. If he is fine, I want to talk to him on the phone." Aveling looked from one to the other but didn't get a reply. "He's dead, isn't he?" she whispered.

"No, sweetheart," her grandmother assured her quickly, "but he is in a very bad way, so his recovery is going to take a little longer."

But Aveling was not to be put off. "Please, Grandma," she pleaded. "I need to see him." Her grandmother sighed. "Look, if you just calm down and stay put today, tomorrow I will arrange for the staff to wheel your bed down to see him. For now, you have to concentrate on your own recovery. If anything happens to you, how am I going to explain that to Lee?"

But the next day it was Aveling who was causing concern. Her condition had deteriorated and she was slipping in and out of consciousness. The prince was in her room, waiting on Madam Aveling returning from a coffee break, when suddenly the girl's heart stopped for no reason.

In his army days, the prince had witnessed similar situations where it wasn't the injury to soldiers that killed them but the aftershock. Before the hospital staff could respond to the alarm from Aveling's monitor, he started CPR, and by the time the crash cart arrived her heart was beating again.

Madam Aveling was shocked when she returned to the room, saw her granddaughter hooked up to even more machines, and heard what had happened. She had been concerned about Lee, but now she was even more worried about Aveling.

For the next few days, the girl slipped in and out of consciousness, and every time she woke up, she kept insisting she should be moved to Lee's room. It was another four days before Lee himself finally came round, and his first words were, "How is Aveling?"

Later that evening, when both patients were asleep, the prince suggested the best medicine might be to move them into the same room. With the help of the staff, the beds were moved to a private room, and the prince and Madam Aveling returned to their hotel hoping to get some well-earned rest.

The following morning, when they returned to the hospital, they found Aveling propped up telling Lee stories about how she had never learned to cook, because the first time she tried she had burned the toast and the boiled eggs were cooked for so long they were like rubber.

Lee was begging her to stop, because it hurt every time she made him laugh and he was worried his stitches would burst.

It was another two weeks before Aveling could leave the hospital, while Lee needed to stay another week. Reluctant to leave without him, Aveling was only finally convinced when he asked her to get some shopping gifts for him to take back to the staff at the castle.

*

When Lee was finally discharged from the hospital, he was still having difficulty walking and, to his annoyance, needed to use a wheelchair. The prince had advised Madam Aveling that it might be better not to fly back to England straight away in case either of the patients needed extra medical help. So, she booked them all on a cruise ship, which would take a lot longer but would give 'the kids' – as she now called them – some recuperating time. And if they needed any medical help, she had engaged a private doctor to travel with them.

Lee and Aveling had never been on a cruise ship and were understandably excited. But any ideas of a relaxing journey to soak in some sun and relax seemed unlikely when Aveling started racing around the deck on the first day, pushing Lee in his wheelchair.

The prince and Lee were sharing a room, so that the older man could keep a close eye on him. After dinner on their last evening, Lee was over-tired, so the prince convinced him to return to the room and get a good night's rest.

Once everybody had gone to their rooms and the lights had been turned out, Aveling was still feeling hyped up. Sleep was the furthest thing from her mind. After staring up at the ceiling for ages while her grandmother snored gently, she redressed and decided to take a walk around the ship.

As she approached the end of the deck, she could see a shadow leaning up against the railing. Unwilling to face an encounter with another strange man, she turned to go in the opposite direction. But as she did, the shadow turned around and called her name.

"Aveling, is that you?"

Rubbing her eyes to focus on the man walking towards her, she still couldn't place him.

When he stopped a few feet away, he said, "I thought it was you when I saw you charging around the deck the other day."

Aveling thought she knew the face but still could not put a name to him, then he introduced himself. "It's me. Luke. We met on the plane from China to England a while ago."

"Oh my, that must have been well over a year ago," she laughed, remembering the young man she had chatted to. "How on earth did you remember me?"

"Silly girl, I knew on that flight we would meet again," he told her. "I also promised myself if we ever did, one of the first questions I would ask is if you'd marry me."

Shocked at his words, Aveling took some time to reply. "Luke," she told him, "I am not that same person anymore. I am on this ship because my grandmother wanted us to recover after some issues we had in China." She didn't want to go into detail about the shooting in the Embassy, or what had happened to her in England and in China.

"I saw you earlier, charging around with the lad in a wheelchair." Luke looked down at her hand, and added, "While I don't see a ring on that finger, I still stand a chance."

Luke went on to ask many questions – some she answered, others were just too painful. But when she told him she had almost died in the Embassy shooting, he grabbed her by the hands and asked if the young guy in the wheelchair had been the other victim.

CHAPTER 17: ONBOARD

"Yes," she confirmed. "We are both just recuperating." Before he could ask anything else, she told him, "This is bizarre. First we meet on a plane – and how on earth you remembered me is mind boggling – but now we meet again on a ship. Why are you here?"

"I'm escorting some goods back to England, and flying could damage the cargo."

Intrigued, Aveling asked what the cargo was, but Luke quickly glanced at his watch without replying. "Sorry," he told her. "I have to go check on that cargo. It's already two am, and they need feeding."

He pulled out a pen and scrap of paper and asked for her number and address, desperate not to lose touch this time.

Knowing how private Madam Aveling was, she said she couldn't give him her address because she lived with her grandmother, but she did give him her mobile number. But she wasn't convinced she would ever see or hear from him again.

When she went back to bed and tried to sleep, her mind kept going over what kind of cargo would need feeding, and why a cruise ship would be used to transport it. It seemed like minutes later that she opened her eyes to find the sun streaming in.

"Morning, lazy bones!" Lee wheeled himself into her cabin. "You better get up or you'll miss breakfast."

After breakfast they all had to do their final packing, but Aveling was hoping to see Luke before she left the ship. Without telling the others, she went off to look for him, only to get lost in the lower decks. Totally disorientated, she had to ask a cleaner who was vacuuming how to get back to her cabin.

By the time she got there, the others were ready to leave and waiting anxiously to disembark.

"Where have you been? I was getting worried," her grandmother said.

But before she could reply, the prince urged, "Come on, slow coach, the car is waiting for us."

Madam Aveling had sent a message for her driver James to come and pick them all up from the ship. On the long journey home, everyone was quiet in the car. All Aveling could think about were the odds of seeing Luke again. In the meantime, until Lee got back on his feet, she was going to make it her responsibility to look after him. She felt guilty that she was the one who had put him in danger.

*

After two months of physio and rehab, Lee was finally back walking. But once he began helping out again on the farm, Aveling felt a little lost. Each day she would ask James if there had been any calls for her, but the answer was always no.

Eventually, James discreetly asked Madam Aveling why her granddaughter was waiting for a phone call. "It must be important," he said, "as she asks me the same question every day."

This was the first Madam Aveling had heard of it, and she could only think the girl must be missing her father or hoping to hear from one of her schoolfriends.

The following month was Aveling's eighteenth birthday, and her grandmother was keen to celebrate the occasion. But she knew Aveling had hated birthday parties since she was a child, which probably started when her mother left and never got back in contact.

It was another hot day on the estate. Lee had already left the castle before Aveling got out of bed, but after her usual mid-morning tea with her grandmother, she decided to go and look for him.

Her grandmother explained that it was not a good idea as the fields he was working on were about five miles away. Aveling was surprised at how big the estate was, as she had never given it a second's thought.

After they'd finished their tea, her grandmother retired to her office with the prince. James was working in the kitchen with the housekeeper, so the afternoon was dragging by. Thoroughly bored, Aveling decided she would go looking for Lee, as she would only have to walk one way then come back on the tractor with him.

The weather that day was perfect, with only a light breeze. As she walked across field after field, she occasionally stopped to just listen to the birds, enjoying the peace. In the distance she saw the tractor, but there didn't seem any point in calling Lee's name when she was so far away.

When she finally reached the tractor, though, it was empty, so she headed towards an old barn where there was another tractor with its bonnet up. Just off the barn there was a small house for one of the estate families, with a small annexe behind, where one of the workers lived.

Aveling had only met Tom once, when Lee had introduced them some time ago. The same age as her, he looked very muscular but quite girlish, with blond curly hair.

As neither he nor Lee were in the barn, she reckoned they must be close by, so she stood on tiptoe to peer in the first window of the annexe. But to her surprise, Tom and Lee were naked on the bed, having sex.

For some reason she couldn't understand, Aveling was angry, and she hurried back across the fields in the hope that no-one would know she had been there. She was sure if they had caught her, they would have been angry and would want to keep her quiet. Lee had a very comfortable life at the castle, and Aveling was certain her grandmother intended to take care of him in her will, but she knew Madam Aveling would be shocked.

As she ran towards the boundary and through the woods, her mind ran riot, wondering if she had missed any signs that Lee was gay. He had put his arm around her in the cave to prevent her from falling, he had kissed her on the cheek back at the old farmhouse, he had even stood in front of a bullet for her! How could she tell her grandmother what she had seen?

Her head spinning, Aveling reached the road and scanned the horizon for the castle. It was huge, yet she could see nothing but farmland around her. She continued walking till she felt a pain in her left foot, and when she sat on a boulder at the side of the road and removed her shoe, there was a very uncomfortable blister.

The sun was beating down and the tarmac looked as though it was about to melt, so she limped along the verge on the side of the road, making slow progress.

When a car pulled up alongside her and she realised it was the prince, she had never been so relieved. He'd been in town for a meeting with his solicitors that afternoon and was heading back to the castle.

Leaning over to open the door for her, he asked, "What on earth are you doing here, young lady? You're miles away from the castle."

"I know," she grumbled. "I decided to take a walk and got totally lost."

He smiled. "Good job I found you. Your grandma must be worrying about you."

When they got back to the castle, Madam Aveling was relieved to see the prince pulling up in his car and her granddaughter climbing out.

"Where have you been?" she asked sternly. "I thought you'd maybe decided to go and find Lee, but he got back ages ago."

"Sorry, Grandma. I just went for a walk and thought I would be able to find my way back, but I got lost."

Madam Aveling shook her head. "Oh Aveling, your sense of direction is hopeless. Never mind, it's almost dinner time."

As they all sat down to eat that evening, Aveling decided she wasn't going to give any indication about what she had seen earlier that day. But when Lee informed Madam Aveling he would still be working over on the back fields again in the morning, her grandmother suggested Aveling might want to join him.

Before he could reply, Aveling interrupted. "It's ok, thanks, I've got plans for tomorrow." She ignored the strange look Lee gave her. "On the road today I saw such lovely scenery that I thought how great it would be to paint it. I've got some art materials in my room, so I think I'll do that tomorrow."

As she lay in bed that night, Aveling began to wonder if Lee had ever said anything to the late duke or her grandmother about his choice of partners. *Maybe he wasn't being honest with them at all, and maybe he had just found himself a very comfortable life,* she thought. But why would she think like that when he had just saved her life?

CHAPTER 18: ARTWORK

After a couple of hours tossing and turning, Aveling still could not get to sleep. Eventually she decided to go along the corridor and talk with her grandmother.

As she approached the bedroom, there was light showing under the door so her grandmother must still be awake. Aveling tapped lightly on the door and heard her grandmother say, "Come in."

Madam Aveling was sitting up in bed reading. "Now, Aveling, what can I do for you?"

Unwilling to discuss Lee and what she had witnessed, Aveling decided to save that conversation until she had sorted it all out in her own head. But as she perched on the edge of the bed, she could not find the right words at that time to chat about anything, so she sat in silence until her grandmother asked her if she was alright.

"Sorry, Grandma. I am struggling with so much, I just don't know where to start. I couldn't sleep and just needed someone to talk to."

Her grandmother took her hand and reassured her everything would be ok, and that the words would come when she was ready. To distract her, Madam Aveling began chatting about the people in the local village.

As she listened, Aveling couldn't help but ask, "How do you possibly remember all the shop owners by name, and all the details about their families?"

Before she could reply, there was a small coughing noise from the other side of the bed. Then Prince Antony popped his head up and slid into a seated position. "Right, girls, please can you finish your chattering in the morning?"

Aveling couldn't hide her surprise, but as she looked over at him, he smiled and her grandmother began to chuckle.

"Oh, don't worry about him, he's just my private hot water bottle," she said, and they both started to laugh. "Off you go to bed, Aveling, and we will have another chat in the morning."

With that, Aveling left the room, but she just could not make any sense out of what she had just seen. Her grandmother had always been so upright and honest, yet it looked like she too had been keeping secrets.

At a loss what to think about anything anymore, she put her head down on her pillow and fell fast asleep.

*

The following morning when she arrived downstairs and joined her grandmother in the conservatory, Lee had already left. Over breakfast, the two women chatted about how and where Aveling would get the best art teacher to school her. But it was when the prince joined them that he offered up an idea which made a lot of sense.

With a lot of contacts around the world, he said he knew a perfect teacher who was currently working in Paris.

"Thank you, but no thank you," Aveling said quickly. "I have heard all about French art teachers."

Her grandmother laughed. "So have I, and there is no way I am letting you out of my sight, so France is a definite no-no."

In the end they decided they would try to find a retired female in the local area to teach her, but they all accepted it would take time to find the right person.

When they'd finished eating and Aveling left the room, the prince voiced his concerns about the girl. He said he couldn't put his finger on what was wrong, but something was definitely bothering her.

Madam Aveling agreed. "I haven't said anything to her because I don't want to put any more pressure on her," she confided. "Maybe she is just a little bored."

The prince looked thoughtful. "Why don't we take her on a trip to London as an early birthday treat?" he suggested. "She can get some new clothes and art equipment, or whatever she fancies. And while you girls are shopping, I can catch up with an old friend I haven't seen for a while."

Madam Aveling thought it was an excellent idea, and when they told Aveling later what they had in mind, she seemed pleased. To their surprise, though, she did not suggest that Lee should go with them.

They decided that James would drive them there, and they would take the train back. On her first journey on a train, Aveling had enjoyed looking at the landscape as they travelled. So, she seemed more excited about the train ride than the actual shopping.

As it was her first trip to the capital, they were keen to show her as many of the sights as possible, and what had started out as a three-day trip stretched into a full week. In that time, she saw the Houses of Parliament, the Tower of London, and Buckingham Palace, along with plenty of shopping.

It was when Aveling reached one of the biggest art shops in the city that her eyes really lit up. And as her shopping basket filled up with equipment, the prince suggested it would be better to have everything sent directly to the castle.

While they were booking a delivery date, the prince added more and more items. "As for the canvasses," he told the shop assistant, "you had better send an extra dozen of everything she has asked for."

Bubbling with excitement, Aveling threw her arms around the prince.

"Well now, if that's all I have to do to get a hug, I think we shall have to make this art shop a regular stop whenever we come to visit London," he joked.

Aveling leaned in to whisper to her grandmother that it was the best shopping trip she had ever had, then she realised it was the only proper one she had been on. In China, the only time she had been allowed to go shopping was when the Ambassador's assistant took her out to buy special food for Embassy parties.

Tired but happy, the ladies returned to the hotel, while the prince went off to catch up with his friend.

Sometime later, as they dressed for dinner, Madam Aveling explained that the prince had invited his friend to join them for the meal. Wearing one of the new outfits they had purchased, Aveling was thrilled when her grandmother said she looked wonderful.

"All you need is some nice jewellery," she commented.

Aveling, though, didn't own any items of jewellery. When her mother had left the Embassy, she had taken everything with her, and jewellery was not something Aveling's father had ever bought her. On one occasion she had asked for a watch for Christmas, but instead she had been given a new backpack for her school homework. To make matters worse, one of the Embassy staff who had taken her shopping had purchased the backpack while they were out buying food, so she knew her father hadn't even bought the gift himself.

After the disappointment of that Christmas, Aveling had lost all interest and excitement about the festivities, and in China it was no big deal. So when her grandmother asked her if she had brought any gems with her from China, she explained that she had never owned any.

Surprised, Madam Aveling asked her granddaughter if she would like to have a look at the jewellery she had packed and to choose something to wear that evening.

After half an hour of rummaging excitedly through her grandmother's jewellery box and trying several items on, Aveling sighed. "Grandma, they are all so pretty and I like so many items, but I don't think they would look right on me."

Her grandmother looked at Aveling's outfit then at her jewellery box. Then she took out a simple gold chain with a star hanging down. The front was covered in diamonds, but when Aveling turned it over, there was an inscription: *To my darling little Gemini, the brightest star in all the sky.*

"This one is perfect for you," Madam Aveling told her, "and I would like you to keep it. It was a gift from your late grandfather, but I haven't worn it for such a long time."

"Oh, Grandma, it's perfect," she breathed, as she hung the necklace around her neck. "But who was Gemini?"

Her grandmother smiled. "When I was a young girl and I first met the duke, I would not tell him my real name. At that time I was always told never to speak to strange men, but I used to see him most days as I walked home from school."

"You were still at school when you met Grandad?" interrupted Aveling in surprise. "How old was he then?"

"I didn't know at first, but I found out later he was in his late thirties."

Aveling was shocked. "Wow, that's so old," she said. "Why did he call you Gemini?"

"Well, one late winter evening as I walked home, it was much later than normal because I had been kept back on detention at school. He was always sitting on the same bench just outside the library, but that night it was so very, very cold and I spotted him before I crossed the road. Before reaching the library, I always passed the chip shop. I had very little money and my family were very poor, so I used to deliver newspapers to make a little pocket money." She smiled at the memory before continuing.

"I knew your grandfather would not have eaten that day, so I stopped at the chip shop and picked up some chips and a battered sausage. When I handed them over to him, he smiled, and I remember his hands were so cold that he held his food close to his chest for the warmth. As he slowly ate the food, he pointed to one group of stars in the sky which he told me was the constellation of Gemini.

"I knew nothing about the night sky, but he told me its constellation was the brightest, and after that day he always called me his little Gemini."

"But why was he there, Grandma?"

"After the war, a lot of men had something they call today PTSD. It's when their minds just cannot accept what has happened to them, so they often never returned to their homes, and depression could easily overwhelm them," Madam Aveling explained sadly.

"So Grandad was a tramp?" Aveling prompted wide-eyed.

"That is what I believed back then, but I could not just pass him by without saying hello. I knew I shouldn't, as my mother drilled into us as children never to speak to strange men," her grandmother went on, "but he was still suffering from what had happened to him in the war and always looked so sad.

"It was much later that I found out so many of his friends had died, and he told me he felt responsible. The sadness overwhelmed him, so I would sit and just chat about everything and anything. One day he told me a story about one of his friends who was a duke and had lived on a huge estate, but after his father had died the government took so much money in taxes the man's family had to sell off a huge section of land." She paused briefly. "The man hadn't been back since the war, because his sister still lived on the estate and he could not face her as she had been engaged to his best friend who had died. He knew she would want every detail of her fiancé's death, but how do you explain when someone you love was blown into pieces with a shell from a tank?

"When he told me this, his voice began to break, and I knew then he was talking about himself. So I sat and just let him talk, and after he finished, I gave him a hug and went home. The next day, after I had given it a lot of thought, I decided I knew exactly what I would say to him on my way home from school. It had been a very cold winter's day, and when I saw him he looked frozen. I told him no matter how hard it was for his friend to see his sister, she needed him more than ever. And I said that no matter how hard it was for him, his sister needed to know the truth so that she could come to terms with it.

"I pointed out that the remaining staff at the family's estate were probably all looking forward to the man's return, so he needed to be brave, stand tall, and return to help with the rebuilding of the estate."

Aveling sat quietly, hanging on her grandmother's words as she continued her story.

"But as I looked at him that evening, I wasn't sure he could stand another night outside. Snow had been forecast, and I was so afraid he would freeze to death. I had only been sitting with him for about ten minutes and my fingers were so cold, but I was wearing a pair of mittens my mother had made for me. So I slipped them off and, as I put them on his hands, he smiled at me.

"The next night when I left school, I looked for him, but he was nowhere to be found. I didn't know if he had survived that night or if he had returned home, but it was only later when he saved me from the police…" Madam's voice tailed off for a moment, as though she was reliving a difficult memory. "Anyway, never mind, Aveling. It is getting late, and we need to go down for dinner."

Aveling wanted to know more. "So, what happened next?"

"I'll tell you another time," soothed Madam Aveling. "Let's go and see if the prince is back from his meeting. I don't know about you, but I am hungry."

As they left their room, Madam Aveling knocked on the prince's door but there was no reply, so they continued downstairs. When they reached the dining room, he was sitting at a table with another man, whose back was towards the women. As they got closer, the prince stood and his guest turned to look at the ladies.

When she caught sight of the man's face, Aveling was stunned. It was Luke – the young man she had met on the plane, then again on the cruise! As the waiter pulled out first Madam Aveling's chair then Aveling's, the young girl seemed lost for words.

The prince introduced his friend to her grandmother then to Aveling, and he realised the two young people must have met before. "Am I missing something?" he asked.

"It's ok," Aveling assured him. "I met Luke on the plane when I first returned to England and then again on the ship."

Madam Aveling frowned. "You met on the boat?"

"It was when I was racing around with Lee," her granddaughter explained. "But I do have a question for Luke. I just can't work out what kind of cargo would not be allowed to fly, and which needed around-the-clock attention and feeding."

Luke laughed. "Is that all you have to ask me after all this time?"

Madam Aveling had never met Luke before, but it was clear he was smitten with her granddaughter. He never took his eyes off her and didn't seem to stop smiling.

But it was the prince who answered Aveling's question.

"Luke, being fluent in Chinese, was asked to accompany two very young panda bears over to England with their keeper," he explained. "But at the last minute the flight was cancelled due to the weather. The baby panda bears needed to be kept calm, and it was decided to bring them by cruise ship."

"But why not return them to where they had come from and wait till the weather improved?" asked Aveling.

"Good question," Luke told her. "But in the mountains where they were rescued, there were earthquakes being experienced, so it wasn't safe to return them. As for the weather, it's always too unpredictable."

CHAPTER 19: LOST TRACK OF TIME

Luke asked how her friend was doing and if he had recovered now, but Madam Aveling and the prince were surprised at her blunt answer, considering she and Lee had previously been close, and he had saved her life.

"He's doing ok," was all she said.

Luke explained he was going to be based and working in London for the next year, but he seemed unsure where he would be reassigned after that.

The four enjoyed plenty of light-hearted conversation over dinner, but once they had finished eating the prince glanced at his watch and announced it was past his bedtime.

"Me, too," said Madam Aveling. "We will leave you two youngsters to chat."

Once they had left, Aveling and Luke lost all track of time, and it was almost two am when she finally sneaked into the bedroom where her grandmother was sound asleep.

The following morning when they all went down for breakfast, Luke was already sitting at the table, and he quickly stood up and helped both ladies to be seated.

"Good morning, Luke," Madam Aveling said. "It's a nice surprise to see you again, but what are you doing here?"

"Sorry, Grandma, I invited him. Is that ok?"

NINE YARDS OF SILK AND THREE PIECES OF JADE

"Of course." Madam Aveling turned to look at Luke and asked what his plans were for the day.

"I was hoping with your permission I could take Aveling around the city to see some of the sites I know she will love," he replied. "I've lived most of my life in London, so I know my way around."

With Madam Aveling's consent, after breakfast the two set off. Luke had planned a trip on a ferry boat to take in river views, but the weather was making it difficult to see anything. So, at the first stop, Luke decided they could return another day and head to an art exhibition he had found, which was right up Aveling's street.

After a pleasant day, Luke joined them that evening for dinner, and once again the two young people stayed on chatting when the older members of the party had retired for the evening.

That night, when Aveling returned to the room, her grandmother was still awake.

"What time do you call this, young lady?" she teased.

But suddenly Aveling burst into tears.

"What on earth's the matter?" her grandmother asked. "I thought you two were getting on like a house on fire."

"We did, but when he leaned into kiss me," Aveling sobbed, "I wanted him to kiss me. But I don't know why, I pushed him away."

Her grandmother smiled. "I think maybe you still need some more time before you start another relationship."

Aveling frowned through her tears. "But I haven't had any relationships."

This time it was Madam Aveling who frowned. "I thought you and Lee were an item? In fact, I was surprised when I saw how happy you were to see Luke."

"Lee and I have never had a relationship," Aveling replied. "At first I was so grateful to him for doing what he did to Mary. She deserved it. I knew he had been told about everything that had happened to me, so I thought he liked me when he put his arm around me in the cave. Then he just gave me a kiss on my cheek on the decking, and again when he saved me." Her voice broke a little. "I thought we were going to be a couple, and I believed he was giving me all the right signals, but then…"

Madam Aveling got out of bed and put her arm around the girl. "Sweetheart, I know how confusing these things are, but if Lee has done something to you that is worrying, you need to tell me." Aveling did not know what to say or how to say it. Since she had looked into that annexe window, she had been trying to convince herself that what she saw had never happened.

"What has he done to make you so upset?" Madam Aveling tried again.

Taking a deep breath, Aveling began, "Do you remember the day I got lost when I went looking for him? It was a long walk, and when I saw his tractor I thought I had found him, but he wasn't there. So I walked over to the old annexe… and when I looked in a window, I saw Lee naked on the bed."

"Oh, Aveling," her grandmother hugged her tighter. "I am so sorry. I didn't know he had a girlfriend."

"No, Grandma, you don't understand." Aveling pulled back to look directly at her grandmother's face. "He was naked on the bed with another boy."

For a few moments there was silence. Then Madam Aveling shook her head and replied, "You must have got it wrong, Aveling. If the duke ever knew that, he would have packed Lee's bags and sent him on his way."

But Aveling was adamant. "Think about it, Grandma. Lee is in his twenties, but has he ever brought a girlfriend back to the castle?"

Her grandmother shrugged. "Well, now you say it, I have never ever seen him with a girl."

"After seeing them together, I didn't know what to do," Aveling went on. "I didn't want him to know what I had seen, so I took off through the woods till I reached the road, then I just kept on walking till the prince found me."

"My poor girl, I had no idea," her grandmother soothed. "Let's get packed up in the morning and get back to the castle."

Aveling looked worried. "Grandma, you won't tell him, will you?"

Madam Aveling shook her head. "No, lass, that's one conversation I don't want to have."

*

The following morning after breakfast, they left for the station. Aveling kept looking around, and her grandmother knew who she was looking for, but Luke never showed.

Noticing that the girl seemed tearful, the prince leaned in to Madam Aveling and whispered, "What's wrong?" But she shushed him with a warning look.

When they arrived at the castle, Lee was waiting for them at the gate, a broad grin on his face. But his face fell when Aveling climbed out of the car, grabbed her case, stormed past him, and rushed up the stairs without saying a word to anybody.

"What's wrong?" he asked the prince.

As he didn't know himself, the prince played for time and simply replied, "We will chat later."

That evening, Aveling did not come down for dinner, so her grandmother sent a tray of food up to the room.

As they ate their dinner, the prince, Lee, and Madam Aveling made little conversation, and the atmosphere was very subdued.

When he'd finished eating, Lee suggested he would pop up and see what was wrong with Aveling. But her grandmother was quick to interrupt.

"No, Lee. I think it would be a bad idea. Just leave the girl alone."

Later that evening when the prince and Madam Aveling were alone, she filled him in on the whole situation. Firstly, how Aveling had pushed Luke away, then why she had been so upset every time Lee's name came up.

The prince looked thoughtful. "I never told Luke anything about what had happened to Aveling, so looking back maybe I should have done so. As for Lee, I must admit I am lost for words. How could he lead the girl on when he knew he preferred boys? To be quite honest with you, maybe it's time that young man moved on."

"Oh, Antony, I don't want to think about Lee or Luke right now," Madam Aveling replied sadly. "I need to think about Aveling's eighteenth birthday party. I was hoping to use the big ballroom that hasn't been used since I married the duke. I thought it would have been perfect for a fancy dress party, but now I know she would not want that." She looked at him hopefully. "If you come up with any ideas, please let me know."

"I will give it some thought," the prince told her. "But right now I am thinking how I can help you get rid of Lee."

"Please don't think about that right now," Madam Aveling urged. "He did set up Mary to help me, and he stood in front of bullets for Aveling. If we just get rid of him because of his…" She paused, unable to say any more, but the prince got the message.

*

Over the next few days, everything at the castle seemed to be ticking along normally, and everybody was getting on with their jobs. Madam Aveling was still trying to find an art teacher for her granddaughter, who was cleaning out part of the conservatory where she had been told she could set up the easel and a table to use.

The delivery arrived on time from the art shop, and Aveling was busy getting everything ready and fixing a canvas on the easel when the prince walked in. She hadn't heard him come through the door, so when he spoke to her, the poor girl almost jumped out of her skin,

"Oh, Aveling, I am so sorry. I didn't mean to startle you," he apologised. "I just popped in to see how you were getting on."

Later that evening, over dinner, the prince casually mentioned he had seen the canvas ready for painting, but advised that it might be a good idea if no-one entered the room unless invited, so that Aveling didn't get a fright.

He added that even though he hadn't been particularly good at art at university, he remembered there was nothing more annoying than people interrupting and asking the same stupid questions. So, he suggested the conservatory should be off limits while Aveling was working there.

The following week, Aveling shut herself off from everyone and was so engrossed in her work that she asked her grandmother if she could have her meal sent into her. But she made a point of saying, "Please use Mrs Clark, and don't ask Lee to bring me anything."

Her grandmother agreed. "Of course. I understand. Just ask if you need anything."

CHAPTER 20: CLOAK AND DAGGER

A few days later, Madam Aveling received a phone call from a private number. It was Doctor Valiere asking for a meeting. Although she agreed to meet at the same time and same place as last time, she was intrigued how the doctor had found her number. She had purchased the phone to ring the doctor when she answered the original advert, but hadn't realised that her number would have been stored on the doctor's mobile so she could call her back.

Over the years Madam Aveling had been careful never to let her guard down, so when she told the prince, he insisted she gave him the phone and he would get rid of it. As she had already agreed to the meeting, she decided she would still go ahead. And later that week she had the prince drop her off at the meeting place, then agreed he would park by some trees and if anything looked suspicious he would call her on another mobile. It seemed a little cloak and dagger, but she knew she was still wanted by the police.

As autumn was getting closer, the nights were drawing in, so it was quite dark when they arrived. The prince and Madam Aveling took a good look around before she finally climbed out of the car and made her way inside the old mill.

A few minutes later, Dr Valerie's son Tommy turned up, and Madam Aveling stepped out, still glancing around her. "What can I do for you, Doctor?"

"My apologies, Madam Aveling, but I know it's your granddaughter's birthday next week and I was hoping you could give her a gift from me," he began.

"Is that all you have called me for?" Madam Aveling was surprised. Looking more closely at him, she realised he seemed very nervous.

Over the years Madam Aveling had become good at reading faces, but she wasn't sure if he was just nervous meeting her or if it was something else. If this was a trap, she had walked right into it, and it was too late to react.

Keen to leave, she held out her hand to receive the gift then turned away to return to her car. But as she walked back to the roadside, Tommy was just a few paces behind.

Stopping, she turned towards him. "Now, young man, if you don't have anything else to say, I will be on my way."

He cleared his throat nervously. "Actually, I was hoping you would give Aveling a message from me. I should very much like to see her again."

Madam Aveling shook her head. "My apologies, Tommy, but that is not a good idea." When he asked for her granddaughter's phone number, Madam Aveling realised he was not going to give up.

But she also knew that any relationship between them would be a disaster. He was older than Aveling, but what worried her more was her own connection with his grandmother, and she could not risk him bringing up her past. If Dr Valerie had any old information on her and passed it on to Tommy, it could be a problem.

She pulled a whistle from her coat pocket and blew it. Suddenly, as if from nowhere, a group of men seemed to surround them. But it wasn't the police. These were ex-military men who she employed to work and live on her estate. Two particular officers lived in a part of the castle, but they all knew how to take care of Madam Aveling – and she looked after them.

The arrival of the men startled Tommy, so Madam Aveling tried to put him at ease a little.

"I will give my granddaughter your gift," she said kindly, "but never call me again unless you or your grandmother are in danger." And with that, she turned and walked towards her car.

CHAPTER 21: BIRTHDAY GIRL

When Tommy returned to his grandmother's home that evening, he stormed in, slamming the door behind him and threw his keys down on the side table in the hall.

He stormed into Doctor Valerie's office and sat down, his face like thunder. "That bloody woman," he fumed. "All I wanted was to see Aveling."

"Tommy, what on earth have you done? When you asked me to set up the meeting, I believed you had some medical notes to discuss with Madam Aveling."

"No," he admitted sheepishly. "I just wanted to give her a gift to pass on to Aveling." Then he explained how he had been surrounded by Madam Aveling's men, who had appeared from nowhere.

His grandmother tutted. "You silly boy, you have no idea who you are dealing with."

She went on to explain how and where she had first met Madam Aveling and revealed that she had made tape recordings during that time. After she retired, Doctor Valerie could never get those taped conversations out of her mind, so to keep herself busy she wrote a book about Madam Aveling's life, entitled *Damaged Mind*.

"I know I should never have done it, Tommy," she admitted, "and I had no intention of sharing it with anyone. But a few years ago your uncle found the manuscript in my drawer and decided to get it published as a surprise for me." She sighed deeply. "Honestly, I would never have written it if I'd thought for one minute it would turn into a best seller. It was hard to keep it from our family members, but I was so ashamed. I should never have used those tapes."

"I don't understand. Grandma," Tommy questioned. "If she was guilty of any crimes, surely the police would have recaptured her before now. And anyway, my understanding was that after twenty years a crime is no longer an issue."

Doctor Valerie shook her head. "Not if the crime is murder." Seeing the shock on his face, she continued, "I think the best thing for me to do is to give you this, then maybe you will understand." She reached into a locked drawer, took out a book, and slid it across her desk to him.

Over the next few days, Tommy found himself engrossed in the story his grandmother had written. When he reached the end, he sought her out and found her busy in her office.

"You are right, Grandma, you should never have written it," he told her. "Do you know if Madam Aveling has read it?"

She shrugged. "That, Tommy, is my worst nightmare."

"Do you believe everything she said on those tapes, or could she have been blowing things up out of all proportion just to get attention?" he asked.

"No." Dr Valerie was adamant. "Reading people's minds was all part of my job, and I do believe every word on those tapes is sadly true."

*

At the estate, the prince had gone back to London, Lee was busy in the fields, Aveling was painting in the conservatory, and her grandmother seemed to spend a lot of time in her office.

After she had finished her work one afternoon, Madam Aveling decided to pay her granddaughter a visit. She didn't want to distract the girl, but she was hoping Aveling would give her some idea as to how she would like to spend her birthday.

As she began the long walk to the conservatory, she saw Lee heading in the same direction, carrying a bunch of wildflowers. Before he could open the door, Madam Aveling called out his name and asked where he was going.

"I thought these would be perfect for Aveling to paint," he explained, holding out the flowers.

"Yes, they are lovely, but I promised Aveling that no-one would interrupt her when she was painting. Why not give them to me? I will put them in water and give them to her later."

He handed over the flowers with a disappointed look, then Madam waited till he disappeared round a corner before she entered the conservatory.

Trying to stay as quiet as possible, she placed the flowers down on the table, but her granddaughter must have heard something, as she turned away from her painting, smiling when she realised who had come in.

Madam Aveling walked over to look at the canvas, then took a big step back. "Oh my goodness, Aveling, that is stunning," she breathed. "I don't think you need any lessons if you can paint like that."

"Thank you, Grandma." Aveling looked delighted. "I was going to ask you if I could have the keys for the back storeroom, as I remember seeing some very old items that would make great still life paintings. If my memory serves me right, there was a very old bird in a cage." Her grandmother laughed. "Oh yes, I had forgotten all about that. I used to love it when it was working, but I think I wound it up too often. When it broke, I remember asking your grandfather if he could get it mended for me, but I think he just forgot. Once you dig it out, I will get James to send it off to get repaired."

CHAPTER 22: NEVER SAY NO

Tommy could not give up on seeing Aveling. She had taken over his heart, and all he could think of was where was she, was she safe, was she being looked after? He was well and truly besotted with the girl.

It had taken him over three days to read the book *Damaged Mind*, then his grandmother had allowed him to listen to the tapes to see if he agreed that Madam Aveling's comments had been genuine.

"You were right, Grandma," he told her when he'd finished. "I wanted to read the book quickly, but I found things were just too horrific and I had to keep putting it down. Then when I heard the tapes, I had to replay some bits then take another break. How people can be so cruel."

Doctor Valerie looked surprised. "Surely doing your job you must have heard worse things?"

"No," he assured her. "This was far worse than anything I have had to deal with in the past; in parts it's just so unbelievable. When you were writing it, surely you must have made it worse just to—"

She interrupted, "No. Your uncle had a few problems getting the book printed due to the ages of the girls, so the publisher made the girls older. I know how shocked anyone would be just listening to the tapes, but remember that back in the sixties things were so very different,"

Just listening to the first tape, Tommy had ended up with tears running freely down his face, but he knew he needed to hear them all to get a better idea of what had been going on in Madam

Aveling's mind. By the time he had finished, all he wanted to do his wrap his arms around her and hug her.

Despite the book and the tapes and his better understanding of Madam Aveling, Tommy still could not get her granddaughter out of his mind. He needed to see Aveling.

*

The encounter with Tommy – and the incident with Harry – had made Madam Aveling aware that her granddaughter would rarely be out of danger, so she considered getting someone to give the girl self-defence lessons. Somehow, though, it didn't seem right for Aveling as she was such a gentle soul.

Madam Aveling thought back on how she had been raised, and how the only thing at the end of the day she could rely on was herself. When she wanted someone dead, they just had to die. Aveling was totally different, but perhaps she could teach her granddaughter something to protect herself.

The next time Aveling went to her bedroom, Madam Aveling followed her. She knew that was the best place for them to talk, as the doors and walls were thick so no-one should overhear them.

She started by asking Aveling a lot of questions to find out just wat she would do if she was ever attacked again. Aveling admitted she wished she had killed "him" the first time he raped her, and her grandmother knew exactly who she was talking about. So she asked the girl how and what she would have used to achieve that.

With a blank expression on her face, Aveling asked, "What would you have done, Grandma?"

"First of all, the moment he used his force on me, in my mind I would know he had to die," her grandmother replied. "So the second he turned away from me, I would have picked up the heaviest thing I could find and smashed it over his head. And if that didn't kill him, I would have hit him again. If that was your only option, you would need to hit him as hard as you could with all your strength, because the last thing you would want is for him to get back up again. An injured animal is harder to handle. If he was unconscious, I would have to finish the job, as dead bodies can tell no tales."

Madam Aveling continued with little emotion, "When he was dead, I would make sure I did not leave any fingerprints. Back in the sixties, things were different, but today you have DNA so it is a little more difficult. But it is easier to act before he hurts you, if you know how. And that's what I will show you… but only if you want me to."

"Yes please, Grandma." Aveling was tearful. "I felt so helpless and I didn't know what to do."

"The first thing is to avoid being in any room with a man if he makes you feel threatened and if he makes any moves towards you. Once he puts his hands on you, you have the right to take defensive action," Madam Aveling explained. "Even now, when I leave the house, I always have at least one aerosol of mace with me, but I also have what I call my fruit peeler knife with me. Over the years I learned when and where and how to use it, but I don't think that's for you. I could be wrong, though. How do you feel about blood?"

Aveling shrugged. "I don't mind blood. It doesn't bother me."

"Well, I will show you how to use a knife to make the best moves. When you have made the choice to cut someone, you need to know where all the main arteries are. It's always been my code to make the fewest cuts, because any attack takes time. Staying calm is also something you need to do."

Aveling listened carefully to hear grandmother's words.

"If your attacker is standing, I would go first for the artery in the left side of the neck. Hold your weapon firmly, then strike with force." She paused for a moment, clearly thinking. "When we can get a little time alone together in the kitchen, I will show you what it feels like to cut a piece of uncooked meat, so you can feel the texture. It's not so different if you cut a man or an animal.

"If you cannot reach the neck, go for the inside top of the left leg. Again, use the knife with confidence and cut deep. I will show you how and where to hit the femoral artery in the leg, as I believe it takes just four minutes to bleed out, which means your victim will not have time to retaliate.

"I will teach you these things, Aveling, but there are some basic things you need to know. Never look anything up on the internet, and never ask anyone else about anything I teach you. And if ever you are picked up by the police, deny everything. Make sure you know your solicitor and legal team's phone numbers but tell them as little as possible. And even when you are as guilty as hell, never tell them you are guilty."

Her grandmother was warming to her subject. "Trust me, these people always chat among themselves, and I know that through experience. On one occasion I was working in a restaurant, and I saw a solicitor who was supposed to be helping me having dinner with the judge. They chatted away when I was close enough to hear a part of the conversation, but at no point did they ever even look up at the girl serving them. Before they left that evening, they had already decided I was guilty, and I would be going directly from the courtroom to prison."

*

Madam Aveling had decided to have a small dinner party with only a few close friends to celebrate her granddaughter's birthday. With everything the girl had been through, she thought it best to keep the guest list to Prince Antony, Lee, the housekeeper James, who was more like a family member than staff, and – they hoped – the prince's brother Pip. He intended to fly in, depending on the weather.

On the morning of her birthday Madam Aveling presented her with a beautiful pearl and diamond tiara. And while she hugged her grandmother and thanked her for such a lovely gift, Aveling wasn't sure where she would ever wear it.

For the rest of that morning, Aveling kept going to the castle gates, where she would stand a while just looking down the road. On one of those visits, Prince Antony drove up and stopped the car.

"Are you waiting for me to get back, Aveling?" he asked. "I promised I would be home in time for your birthday."

Then he noticed tears in her eyes, so he climbed out of the car and hugged her. "This is no way to celebrate your birthday. Why are you waiting at the gatehouse?"

"I was looking for the postman," she sobbed. "I was hoping my dad or mum would send me a card. I know they often forget, but today I am eighteen." She looked at him hopefully through her tears. "Do you think they are going to surprise me and turn up later?"

"I really could not say," replied the prince, "but someone has remembered. Look up there." It was Prince Pip arriving in his helicopter.

Antony told Aveling to jump in his car and they would cut across the field to meet his brother, and as they stood and watched the helicopter landing, he offered her his hanky to dry her tears.

When Prince Pip climbed out, he was not alone. He had stopped off south of London to take on fuel and to pick up his passenger

– Luke, who had the biggest smile on his face the second he saw Aveling.

He moved in just to give her a hug and kiss for her birthday, but he was beaten to the post as Prince Pip had already grabbed her.

"I have heard all about you from my brother," the dashing prince said. "But he never said you had come down from heaven and God is missing one of his angels."

Everyone laughed then they set off towards the castle. Aveling was walking beside Luke, chatting with him. But Prince Pip had never met her before and could not take his eyes off her.

Prince Antony, who was twenty-five years older than his brother, noticed the look on Pip's face. "Take your eyes off her," he warned. "I know what you are thinking, and she is too young for you."

As Pip seldom took any advice from his brother, Prince Antony began to worry about inviting him for the celebration. But he had been such a good sport to help with the setup of the Glenhall wedding that he'd been keen to include him.

When they reached the castle entrance, James was waiting to show Pip and Luke to their rooms, while Aveling very excitedly ran into her grandmother s office.

The office was large, with a gothic fireplace boasting a roaring fire most of the year, burning wood from the estate. Aveling plonked herself into one of the huge armchairs beside the fire as her grandmother looked up with a welcoming smile.

"Where have you been hiding yourself this morning? I was looking forward to seeing you, to finish the menu for tonight. But not to worry, I have finished it."

The setting chosen for dinner that day was to be the round table in the small dining room. So now it would be Pip, Antony, Luke, Madam Aveling, Lee, James, and the birthday girl. To her grandmother's delight, Aveling seemed to be smiling properly for the first time in ages.

Later that day, when dinner was just thirty minutes away, Madam Aveling went to her granddaughter's bedroom. When she entered, Aveling looked at her in amazement. The older lady looked like something from a story book, wearing a full-length gown and a coronet with diamonds that dazzled under the light.

"Have you not decided which dress to wear tonight?" she asked Aveling.

"No, Grandma." Aveling looked stressed. "You have bought me so many, I just seem to be overwhelmed. Can you pick one for me?"

After a quick flick through the hangers in the wardrobe, Madam Aveling decided on a full-length shimmering gold dress. "Now," she added, "I saw your face this morning when I gave you the tiara. So tonight is the best time to put it to use."

Once she was dressed and the tiara sitting perfectly on her head, Aveling and her grandmother looked into the full-length mirror together, smiling broadly at what they saw. Madam Aveling felt so proud of everything her granddaughter had come through, and she was determined tonight would be a very special evening.

Downstairs, the five gentlemen all stood as the ladies entered the room. Luke moved to Aveling's chair to help her, while Prince Antony as always assisted Madam Aveling. The room had been lit by candles, and the diamonds the two ladies wore shone like stars in the sky.

For her part, Aveling was a little overwhelmed at the attention. Prince Pip, Luke, and Lee all kept asking her questions, barely giving her time to catch her breath between courses.

When the dinner was drawing to close, Prince Antony stood up and said he had an announcement to make.

CHAPTER 23: THE ROYALS

"While I was away, I went to see my father," he told everyone. "As most of you here know, my older brother Michael, my younger brother Prince Pip, and I have never had any children of our own. Although my father is still hoping Pip will make him a grandfather," he added looking towards the younger prince. His brother immediately glanced at Aveling.

"Anyway, my father agreed that I could adopt a granddaughter." Prince Antony looked at Aveling. "So, young lady, this is our birthday gift for you. How would you like to be a real princess?"

Stunned, Aveling turned immediately to look at her grandmother, who smiled and nodded her head. "Is that possible?"

Prince Antony nodded. "We have talked with the solicitors and a whole team of barristers, and everything has been settled. All you have to do is say yes and sign this paper."

Bubbling with excitement, she took the papers he offered and quickly signed her name. She didn't know if it was real or not, but she was thrilled that everyone had gone to so much trouble to make her birthday happy.

Luke's gift was wrapped in the most beautiful paper, and she slowly opened it to find a lovely white gold chain with a stone she had never seen before, but which he explained was a cabochon yellow beryl. Smiling, she leaned over to kiss his cheek. As she did so, she noticed Lee looking on as if someone was stealing his girl, which made her feel uncomfortable but she wasn't going to let it spoil her night.

Next, Prince Pip stood up and passed a shoe box-sized parcel across the table. Aveling opened it up to find another wrapped box inside, then she giggled to find another box inside, then another. When she finally opened the last box, she found a set of keys on a keyring with a Porsche logo.

Bewildered, she looked up at the prince. "Thank you, but I don't know how to drive."

"Don't worry about that. I will start giving you lessons in the morning."

Beaming, Aveling went round the table to give him a hug and kiss him on the cheek. But as she moved towards him, he turned his face so that the kiss ended on his lips. It took her by surprise, but he just laughed, "Got you!"

His brother was quick to notice how flustered Aveling looked. "Pip," he warned, "leave the poor girl alone. She is not used to people like you."

At that moment, the door opened and one of the staff entered. The man went directly to Prince Antony and whispered in his ear. Madam Aveling was intrigued, as the staff would normally speak to her first. But while the servant was speaking, two smartly dressed men came into the room, followed by two police officers in uniform.

The older of the plain clothed men asked to speak with Madam Aveling, who stood up from the table. But as she did so, one of the uniformed officers approached her, saying she was under arrest for murder and immediately placed handcuffs on her. The officers then made to lead Madam Aveling out of the room, while Prince Antony demanded to know what the charges were, and Prince Pip held back Lee and Luke who were ready with their fists.

Within minutes, Madam Aveling was bundled outside and into a car then driven off, leaving the birthday girl sobbing and pleading for them to bring her grandmother back. Luke quickly wrapped his arms around her, but Lee tried to pull them apart and the whole evening just seemed to explode.

As Aveling screamed and wailed, Prince Antony was on the phone. After a few minutes, he gave Prince Pip some instructions then picked up his car keys and left the castle. It was left to Prince Pip to try to explain the situation to Aveling.

"Your grandma would not like to see you like this," he soothed. "But please don't worry, your grandfather has got this."

Aveling shot him a confused look through her tears. "My grandfather?"

"Do you remember the papers you signed earlier this evening?" he went on. "You are now one of us – a princess. A royal princess. But that's because your grandmother is also one of our family. I know she didn't want anybody here to know, but it's unavoidable now. Your grandmother married my brother seven years ago back in my country, in a very small, private ceremony. So I know he will not come back without her. I know him well enough to be sure that he will do everything in his power to bring her back home."

*

When Madam Aveling was led into the police station, she caught sight of Dr Valerie's son Tommy in the corridor. By the time the prince arrived, she was about to be charged with a huge list of crimes.

But before they could take her fingerprints, Prince Antony stormed into the room with his barrister, who immediately insisted they had the wrong woman.

Ignoring the denials by the two detectives, the barrister continued, "If you wish to address this lady, I would be most grateful if you would use her correct title of royal princess." Noticing their confused looks, he went on, "So, do you have any proof?"

At that point, a senior officer entered the cramped room and apologised for any mistake made by his staff, although they still maintained they had the right woman.

The barrister turned to Madam Aveling, who looked totally out of place in a police station, wearing a tiara and evening gown. But as always, she kept a calm attitude, and her face gave nothing away as she agreed to have her fingerprints taken.

However, once the results were fed into the computer, the senior officer returned to inform them they were not a match for anything on the police system. He told them to release the princess immediately, and Madam Aveling, Prince Antony, and the barrister wasted no time in leaving the police station.

As they reached the door, Tommy was still shouting and demanding that they had the right woman. But the barrister paused briefly to inform him that if he continued to make such ludicrous and slanderous accusations, they would be more than happy to see him in court.

When they got back to the castle, Aveling was still pacing up and down in her grandmother's office, watched by Prince Pip and Luke. Lee had left, but no-one seemed to know where he had gone.

Once she had hugged her granddaughter and assured her she was fine, Madam Aveling told her everything had been just a silly mistake. Then she ushered the exhausted girl up to her bedroom, while the men waited downstairs.

When Aveling was settled and almost asleep, Madam Aveling returned to her office to join the others. Her husband and Prince

Pip already knew everything, but Luke was still in the dark and asked if someone could please explain what had happened.

It was almost three o'clock in the morning, so Prince Antony started to share some of the story, but not all, and explained that Madam Aveling had a very interesting but not to be spoken about past.

Luke asked, "But if the police did have the right woman, how on earth did you get her released – and so soon?"

"All we can tell you at this moment is that Madam Aveling's late husband, the duke, brought her to our city to have some surgery. He and my father had attended university in England together, although they had not been in contact for many years." He paused briefly. "The duke asked for help to get the surgery for Madam Aveling, but it had to be under another name. And that is when she had her fingerprints burned off by a very skilled surgeon, who then created new prints for her and made some minor changes to her face. While she recovered, they stayed with our family for the whole summer, and after that I became a regular visitor and stayed with the duke and Madam Aveling if I was in England on business."

Luke still looked a little bewildered at the explanation but listened carefully as the older man continued.

"Madam Aveling was still in her teens at that time, and the duke was over twenty-five years older. Over the years he put in place a background story for her, backed up with all the necessary paperwork that would keep MI5 and the best minds in the country a lifetime to crack. So, we are trusting you to keep this information to yourself."

Once Madam Aveling and Luke had gone off to bed, Prince Antony took the opportunity to talk to his brother alone. He was worried about the looks Pip had been giving Aveling and was keen to give him some advice. But it didn't go as he expected. The younger prince told him to back off and added that for the first time in his life he was sure he was in love.

"I didn't want to be," he told Prince Antony, "but the second I saw her, I was totally captivated, and I just want to love and protect her."

Antony was furious. He knew Pip's history and how he would wine and dine a woman then within weeks have a different one on his arm. "You're too old for her," he snapped as a final warning.

But Prince Pip was quick to remind him that Madam Aveling had been so much younger than the duke. No matter what his brother said, Pip wasn't going to stop going after the girl.

*

The following morning, Lee asked if he could take some time off. But when Madam Aveling asked him why, he said he just needed some time away from work. Without telling her, he decided that he wanted to find out why Aveling was avoiding him.

After breakfast, Madam Aveling and Prince Antony shut themselves away in her office to discuss how to handle Doctor Valerie's son Tommy. Despite all the trouble the young man had caused, she didn't want to take any official action. She believed the best way forward would be to talk to Dr Valerie.

Still concerned, Prince Antony advised her not to ring the woman in case the police had a recording device on the phone. Reluctantly, she agreed, but added that she might have to if everything did not return to normal.

Suddenly Aveling crashed into the office, shouting that Lee and Prince Pip were fighting in the conservatory. But by the time they hurried there, the fight had spilled out into the corridor.

"What the bloody hell do you to think you are doing?" Madam Aveling's voice was cold. "You are upsetting Aveling, and I won't have it."

Prince Antony never said a word, but he pulled his brother to one side. He knew he could never beat his younger brother in a fist fight, but he also knew Pip would never strike him.

Pip spoke first. "We all know not to go into the conservatory when Aveling is painting, but when I was passing, I heard Lee arguing with her," he explained. "He said he loved her, and that she had to stay away from me and Luke. Who the hell does he think he is? The cheek of him when we all know what he did."

Lee retaliated, "And just what the hell am I guilty of?"

At that point, Prince Antony pulled Lee to one side. He didn't want his wife and new granddaughter to overhear the conversation.

CHAPTER 24: I NEVER KNEW YOU

James, the housekeeper, had heard the shouting and arrived in time to overhear part of the conversation and argument. He calmly asked the two princesses to join him in the kitchen so he could make them some tea – something he had always done in the past when Madam Aveling and the duke had words.

After about an hour, Lee stormed into the kitchen. "Aveling, it's not what you think."

She shook her head. "Lee, I saw you with my own eyes."

Lee's shoulders slumped. "I have finished the affair," he told her. "I've never had any feelings for anyone until I met you."

But her grandmother spoke before Aveling could reply. "Look, Lee, the duke always said a leopard never changes his spots." She went on, "At first I thought you might be too old for her, but as you both seemed close and Aveling seemed happy to be with you, I kept an open mind. And when Aveling told me what she had seen, at first I didn't believe it. I know you knew how the duke felt about two men being together, so I can understand why you kept it secret. But," she stressed, "what Aveling saw was unforgivable."

Realising he couldn't win the argument, Lee stormed out, slamming the door behind him.

Just as Prince Antony joined the ladies in the kitchen, his brother came rushing in to speak to him. He pulled Antony into a corner, desperate to make sure Madam Aveling could not use her lipreading skills.

"I went for a walk outside," he lowered his voice to just more than a whisper, "and you will not believe who I have just seen in the grounds."

"Dr Valerie's son, Tommy?" guessed Antony.

Pip shook his head. "Harry. The one Lee beat the hell out of."

Prince Antony was shocked. "How the hell did he get out of prison? And how did he know where to find us?"

Turning to look at his wife, he noticed Aveling was distracted by making more tea. So, he whispered to Madam Aveling what Pip had just told him.

Without reacting, she asked James to take Aveling to the cellar, B1. The castle had six cellars in total, but B1 – where the wine was stored – was the closest to the kitchen and where Aveling would be safe. While she was issuing instructions, Prince Antony called the police.

Madam Aveling knew that if Lee found Harry, he would not be able to control his temper. So, she quickly messaged all the estate workers to find Lee and send him back to the castle.

After a few minutes, he called her to ask why she wanted him to return. But Madam Aveling refused to elaborate and just told him to get back urgently.

With Aveling safely in the cellar, the others gathered in the kitchen, including Lee. At that point, Madam Aveling asked Pip if he was one hundred percent sure it was Harry he had seen.

"Yes, definitely."

Lee immediately demanded to know where he had last been seen. But Madam Aveling shook her head at Pip, so he did not answer.

Madam Aveling began to issue others. "Antony, please stay with me here in the kitchen, to be ready for the police questions. James, stand by the front door but don't open it unless it's the police. Luke, Lee, take the lift up to the roof and you will find binoculars in a locker already up there—"

At that point Prince Antony interrupted. "I think it would be better for me to go up on the roof with Luke, not Lee."

Madam considered his suggestion and looked over at both young men, then she replied, "Ok, you go to the roof with Luke. Lee knows all the entries and exits into the castle, so he would be better to escort the police with the search."

With that, they all headed off.

After at least thirty minutes, the police still hadn't arrived. Suddenly Madam Aveling heard glass breaking, but no-one had alerted them from the roof, so Harry must have got into the outer courtyard before Prince Antony and Luke got up there.

Everything began to happen quickly. Lee took off in the direction of the breaking glass with Madam Aveling following him. She saw Lee open the conservatory door, but Harry must have been hiding behind the hall door, because the next thing she saw was Lee falling flat on his face. As Lee was a well-built young man, Madam Aveling knew he must have been hit very hard.

Although she wanted to dash to Lee's side, something held her back. That was when she heard Aveling's voice and turned to see the girl running towards her.

"No, Aveling, get back! Run!" she shouted.

Before she could turn back to see where Harry was, Madam Aveling was pushed hard, causing her to fall against the wall and land on the floor.

Instead of running away, Aveling was still hurrying towards her grandmother. "No!" Madam Aveling called again. "Run."

But it was too late. Harry grabbed Aveling by the arm and began to drag her back to where he had entered the castle. Slumped in pain in the corridor, Madam Aveling struggled to try and get up, and she could see Lee was still out cold on the floor.

Within minutes, James came rushing to her side, followed by two police officers. Realising what had happened, James called Prince Antony's mobile to let him know the situation and ask Luke to stay on the roof to scan the horizon and grounds and give the police officers the location of Harry and Aveling if he saw them.

James then phoned for an ambulance, and as Prince Antony was examining his wife to see the extent of her injuries, Luke called from the roof.

He had spotted Harry on a quad bike, heading for the gatehouse. The police rushed off in that direction, but by the time they reached the gatehouse, Harry had changed vehicles. With no idea of a make or model, and no registration number, he had got clean away with Aveling.

Everybody was in a state of shock. Lee was taken to hospital, still unconscious, but Madam Aveling refused to leave without news about Aveling.

Throughout that day there were no sightings of Harry. The police sent cars to the Glenhall Estate and to Harry's last address, but there was nothing to report.

The father of the two princes, King Steffon, had only just welcomed his new granddaughter to the family, so when he learned of her kidnap on the news channel, he immediately called Prince Antony.

Although he was in his eighties, he was as sharp as a knife and fit as a fiddle.

When he told his sons he was coming over, they were worried about the press attention and didn't know if it was a good idea. But they knew that if they didn't get Aveling back alive, their father would turn their world upside down to find her attacker.

*

The following day, it seemed as though the police had taken over the castle. They had placed listening devices on the phones, but everyone knew it was a waste of time as Harry had not taken Aveling to ransom her.

Madam Aveling had finally conceded to go to hospital, where it was found she had a broken arm and would need surgery to reset it. The doctors told Prince Antony they needed to keep her in for at least forty-two hours, as she was still in a lot of pain.

Desperate to ensure his wife did not discharge herself, he insisted he had everything under control and that she must stay in the hospital for at least twenty-four hours after the operation. He also persuaded Madam Aveling to stay there by telling her to check on Lee, who was still unconscious.

The following day, there was still no news, but the King had arrived. Within a short time, he was heard shouting at the two princes, but no-one could understand a word he was saying as he wasn't speaking English. When the princes left the room, though, it was clear the conversation had not been a good one.

Antony and Pip wanted to offer a reward for Aveling's safe return, but the police put a stop to it. And when their father heard what they wanted to do, he was enraged. "I thought you two knew better. If you offer any kind of reward, it will be open season on all royal lives!"

"But surely—" Prince Antony began.

"No!" the king interrupted. "If you do that, all the phone lines will light up with everybody saying they know where Aveling is being held, but in reality, they just want the money. Let the police handle this."

With the king's arrival, the press had somehow managed to obtain information about the marriage of Prince Antony and Madam Aveling, which had just added fuel to the fire storm. And with every new revelation, the press pack from all over the world grew larger at the castle gates.

Within days, Madam Aveling was home, Lee had regained consciousness and was recovering at the castle, and all the estate workers were on high alert. Prince Antony reassured his wife they would get her granddaughter back, but he was worried it would all prove too much for her.

And there was still no news.

CHAPTER 25: KEEPING UP

Madam Aveling had always kept up with technology, but she didn't have much information to start with in her search for her granddaughter. All she knew for sure was that Harry had a different car, and regardless of the number of police searching or the constant press stories, there were still no results.

She wasn't sure if Harry had taken Aveling to lock her up somewhere, or if he had taken her to kill her. So, despite the discomfort of her arm being in a plaster cast, she opened her laptop to try and see what information she could glean.

In the forefront of her mind was how on earth this man was allowed to be free. After all, he was guilty of not just rape, but previous kidnapping, yet all the police would say was that he was out on day release from the mental hospital where he had been held since his arrest. When he hadn't returned from his day out, the hospital authorities had lost track of him.

Madam Aveling was annoyed with herself for not properly taking care of Harry herself the first time, and now she was determined she would not allow him his freedom again. First, though, she had to convince everybody she was working with the police, while in reality she had no faith in them. So, she shut herself in her office, working with just the laptop for help.

She knew that Harry would need a car, so she began by searching for every vehicle that had been sold or rented within a five-mile radius of his old home address and a five-mile radius of the castle. He would also need somewhere close to take Aveling, so she messaged all the local estate agents about rental properties and attached a photo of Harry. She knew it was a long shot, but nobody else was coming up with any ideas, and the police thought her suggestions were a waste of time.

By the end of that day she had a list of one hundred and twenty-four cars, which meant she now had to make some guesses. She dismissed all cars sold to women, which took the list down to eighty-nine. As Harry wouldn't want the police to pull him over if they checked registration plates and found he had no insurance, she wondered if he had insured the car in his own name.

There was one detective staying at the castle to monitor the phone lines. And although she didn't want to, Madam Aveling asked if he could get her access to the police site for registration plates. Thankfully, he was only too happy to help,

She knew it would take time to process eighty-nine number plates with the list of insurance companies she gave him, but at that time it was all she had, and several days had already passed with no news.

Madam Aveling knew exactly what Harry was going to do to her granddaughter, but she was so worried that when he finished hurting the girl, he would kill her.

The detective had only been at her computer for a few minutes, when he looked over to Madam Aveling with a smile on his face. He had matched one of the car number plates with a new insurance policy set up in Harry's own name. And he had used an address only ten miles away from the castle.

As he was explaining his find, Madam Aveling received a phone call on her private number from one of the estate agents, giving her an address. And when she repeated it, the detective was reading out the same property.

Immediately, the whole room went silent. Luke muttered, "Oh my god!" The others looked stunned. Madam Aveling was wary of getting too excited, but one tentative lead was better than nothing.

NINE YARDS OF SILK AND THREE PIECES OF JADE

Before Madam Aveling could ask James to bring her car round, the police were already ahead of her. This case had been so big in the press, particularly as it involved the life of a royal princess, that they were conscious of its importance. The detective in the room asked Prince Antony to stay put, keep his wife calm, and stop her from what he said would be interfering with police actions. They had everything under control, he assured them.

But the waiting was driving Madam Aveling mad, and at one point she tried to sneak out of the castle, only to be turned back by the police.

Then out of the blue, the phone rang. It was the police to say they had Harry in custody, and Aveling was doing well but had been taken to the local hospital for a full check-up.

There was no stopping her grandmother any longer. She immediately jumped out of her seat and was already at the front door when Prince Antony caught her.

"No, Aveling, you cannot go to the hospital," he told her.

They were joined by her father-in-law, who repeated the instruction to stay put. He explained that the press camping out at the gatehouse would follow her, so it was better if she stayed home. He added that the police would sneak Aveling out of the hospital once she had been checked over, and bring her home.

"But what will she think if I don't go? And what if they keep her in?" argued Madam Aveling.

"Don't worry, we'll give it thirty minutes then we will phone the hospital." But that time came and went, and when they phoned, they could not get through.

James shouted from the hallway that he could see a van coming up the driveway but its windows were all blacked out, so he couldn't see who was inside. "There are escort cars in front and behind it," he said, "so I think it's got to be Aveling."

Excited now, members of staff started to gather in the forecourt, but the king ordered them all to disperse. "The poor girl has just been through a horrendous ordeal," he told them. "Only Madam Aveling and I will wait here."

When the vehicle pulled up and Aveling stepped slowly out, the king held out his hand to help her out, then her grandmother dashed forward and wrapped her arms around her. It was only then that Aveling saw her grandmother's arm was in plaster.

"Oh, Grandma, your arm! Did he do that to you?"

Madam Aveling smiled without replying then introduced Aveling to her new royal great-grandfather, not knowing what response to expect. But the young girl threw her arms around him, and it seemed like she was never going to let him go.

"My, my, that's the best hug I have had for years," he laughed. "Now, behind that door are rather a lot of people waiting to see you, but I thought it best for just me and your grandmother to welcome you home. I didn't think you would want any fuss."

"I'm just so happy to be home, I want to hug everyone." Aveling smiled broadly.

At that, the king waved his hand and everyone poured out of the building, taking it in turns to hug her or welcome her back.

Once everything had calmed down, the family went back into the castle, and Madam Aveling told the men to leave their questions until later. "Let's all go and freshen up and have dinner in the big dining room."

By the time they all sat down to eat, everyone was being careful not to question Aveling. They did not want to cause her any stress, and her grandmother had made it clear that the subject of the past few days was taboo for now.

*

Madam Aveling had gone to a lot of trouble with the dining room table that evening, with a beautiful centre decoration which was a combination of roses and lilies, its perfume filling the air. The big circular table was one of Madam Aveling's favourite items of furniture in the castle, but it was rarely used. It had incredible carvings of shields belonging to royal families around the world – a different one at each place setting, and a matching shield carved on the back of each chair. The table was mostly covered that evening with placemats and silver.

As she looked around the table, Madam Aveling realised for the first time that there were two princesses present. Since her marriage to Prince Antony, she had never thought of herself as a princess, and when she had returned to the castle after her wedding, she had decided not to tell the staff in case one of them let it slip. The last thing she had wanted was for the press to splash her all over the headlines, and a part of her felt like she was being unfaithful to the old duke by getting married again.

After the meal had finished, the group retired to the far end of the room where there was a huge fire roaring away. The king was chatting to his sons and Madam Aveling, Lee had left the room, and Luke watched as Aveling started to help the staff clear the table. While it was not something one would expect a princess to do, he thought it might take her mind off the past few days, so he took off his jacket to help her.

When most of the dinner dishes were cleared away, Aveling noticed all the decoration around the table and chairs.

"Why are the carvings so deep and different?" she called over to her grandmother.

But it was the king who was quick to respond. "Have you never see it before? Didn't your grandma tell you it's the original round table that King Arthur used?"

Aveling looked at him warily. "Grandad, don't be silly, everybody knows that was just a story; it's not real."

CHAPTER 26: OLD STORIES

This was the first time the old king had ever been called grandad, and everyone looked in his direction as he walked over to Aveling and wrapped his arms around the girl. It was difficult to see if he was crying or laughing, but he held onto her so tightly that eventually she whispered, "Grandad, I can't breathe."

For the rest of that evening everyone was content to sit around the fire just making small talk, and it was almost midnight when James came in to ask if they needed anything else.

As they had been chatting, Aveling had been showing Luke the three pieces of broken jade, but it was then James saw them for the first time. Intrigued, he asked if he could take a closer look.

Realising the time, Madam Aveling suggested that she and her granddaughter should retire for the night. But it wasn't sleep she was thinking about. She had watched Aveling all evening and was concerned that the girl was acting as though nothing had happened.

She also knew her granddaughter would have to make a full statement to the police in the morning, so she was keen to get Aveling alone to offer her some advice.

Before she could ask anything, Aveling jumped in. "It's ok, Grandma, I have it all worked out. This time I followed your advice, and I didn't give that creep time to rape me again." And she went on to describe in detail what had happened that day.

"When I heard all the commotion and shouting, I left the cellar to make sure you were okay," she told Madam Aveling. "On the way, I picked up a fruit knife, like yours, from the kitchen and concealed it inside my cardigan. A lot of the rest of what happened is a blur, but he transferred me from the buggy into the boot of a car, and we seemed to drive for miles off a beaten track. When he let me out of the car, he took me into an old cottage which looked miles from anywhere and tied me up with cable ties then left me alone, The room was cold and damp and had a smell that is still difficult to get out of my nostrils."

She shuddered slightly at the memory then went on, "When he came back to the cottage, it was dark outside. He then dragged me down to a basement and used a chain to attach me to an old radiator."

"Oh my poor girl, you must have been terrified," Madam Aveling told her.

"The next day I never saw him," Aveling went on, "and I knew if I was going to escape I would have to wait till the house went quiet. I could hear him moving about upstairs, so I knew I'd have to wait till he had gone out or to bed.

"When I heard the cottage fall silent, no creaking doors or floorboards, I worked the knife out of my pocket and cut the cable ties off my wrists and my legs. Then I used the point of the knife to unscrew the screws holding the radiator to the wall." She looked sheepishly at her grandmother. "Sorry, Grandma, I did damage the point of the knife."

Madam Aveling patted her hand reassuringly.

"I didn't know how long I had been locked up for, but I crept up the stairs slowly and quietly. I had picked up an old bit of lead pipe before I left the cellar, and I had the fruit knife in my pocket, in case I needed to protect myself.

"When I got to the top of the cellar steps, I found the door locked. But," she grinned, "you would have been so proud of me,

Grandma. I didn't panic. I took the knife out and tried to pick the lock but it didn't work. So I put my shoulder to the door, which must have been very old, and it cracked open.

"I slowly and quietly eased the door open and stepped outside. That's when I started to panic a little, as it was so dark and I didn't know which way to go. There were no street lights anywhere, and the wind was blowing, but I knew if I stayed calm somehow I would be able to get back home. It had to be miles from anywhere, so once I decided on a direction, I started to run at first then walk. I seemed to be going uphill, and after I had been walking for what seemed a lifetime, I could just see the day breaking over the horizon."

She paused briefly before taking up her story again. "I did not know if he had discovered me missing or if he had started to track me down, so I just kept walking, thinking I would come across some signs of life, but I found no-one. Then I heard a car engine getting closer and I was scared it was him.

"I hid behind some bushes, but when the vehicle was almost on top of me, I saw the logo on the side of the vehicle said GPO. So, I jumped out and flagged it down. I think I gave the postman a real fright!" She laughed. "I asked if he could give me a lift down to the village, and he agreed. But when he asked me if I was the missing princess, I don't know why but I just shook my head. I think at that moment I had never been called a princess before so it just didn't register with me. Or maybe it was still in my mind that I could trust no-one.

"The radio was on in his van, and when the news came on, there was a description of my clothing, so the postie turned to take another closer look at me and said, 'Oh yes you are. Wait till I tell my wife. Can I have your autograph for her?'

"It just seemed so surreal. And when we reached the village, the police were everywhere. They helped me out of the van and into a police car, then I saw they were putting the poor postie in handcuffs, so I yelled at them that he was the one who had saved me." She frowned. "I begged them to let him go, but they pushed him into another police car, and as we were pulling away I saw a convoy of police vans heading to the old cottage where Harry had been holding me. I had no idea of the name of the road or anything, as it had been so dark when I left the cottage, but I guess the postie must have told them where he had picked me up, and he probably knew the area well."

"I'm just so glad you're safe, darling," Madam Aveling told her. "And I am incredibly proud of you."

*

The next morning they had barely got out of bed when someone was knocking on the front door. When James opened the door and saw so many uniforms, it was clear this was going to be a difficult day for Aveling. But she had been well coached by her grandmother what to say and to keep her responses fairly brief.

As the day progressed, all the staff were called on individually to provide statements, so everyone was exhausted by the time the police finally left.

The following day, the king was going to return home. But before he left, he called Aveling into the dining room.

What she saw made her recoil in fear, as Harry was sitting at the other side of the table! Her grandfather put a comforting arm around her and led her to the seat opposite Harry. He then sat down on Aveling's left, while Prince Pip and Prince Antony were on her right.

It was clear something was about to happen, and it was the king who spoke first. "Now, Aveling, we all know what he did to you.

So now it's down to you today to decide what—" "Where's my grandmother?" Aveling interrupted anxiously.

"You don't need to worry your grandmother," the king reassured her. "And as for the British police and courts, they have all let you down. So it's up to us to decide what happens now."

"But how did you get the police to release him?" she asked, looking baffled.

"They had their chances to put him behind bars more than once, so I am now going to ask a question that only you can decide the answer. All you need to say is yes or no." The king paused to look at her carefully. "So, Aveling, do you want this man out of your life forever? Yes or no!"

Aveling's mind was in overdrive. She knew if she said no, her family would just hand him back to the British police. But if she said yes, she believed she was signing Harry's death warrant.

When she paused for just a few minutes, Harry began to beg her for his freedom, but she had had more than enough of this man destroying her life. She calmly replied, "Yes, Grandfather. I want him out of my life and mind forever."

The king nodded. "Right. Please understand, Aveling, when you leave this room I do not want you to discuss anything we have said with anyone. And when I say tell no-one, I mean no-one."

Nodding, Aveling got up from her chair and hurried out of the room. She felt as though her legs would give way, and her stomach was cramping up as she gasped for air. It was then Luke spotted her, just as she was about to fall to the floor.

As he lifted her up, the office door opened, and the two princes stepped out, indicating he should get Aveling out of there quickly.

Then three burly security officers pushed past the two princes and walked into the office.

There were some muffled screams, and Luke paused only briefly before helping Aveling into the kitchen.

*

Later that day, after saying her goodbyes with her new great-grandfather, the castle seemed so very quiet. The two princes were out on the estate with the groundsman and Luke, getting ready for the shooting season. Madam Aveling was working in her office, while Lee was at the furthest away fields.

Aveling headed for the conservatory to return to her painting, but her mind would not settle. She kept asking herself if she had done the right thing or not. *No matter how cruel Harry had been, did he deserve to die?* she wondered.

She looked up at the clock. It was almost four, so it was time to get washed up for tea. As she walked down the corridor, she ran into her grandmother leaving her office. Immediately sensing the girl was troubled, Madam Aveling asked if she was alright.

Immediately tears filled young Aveling's eyes, and she started to tell Madam Aveling what she had said and done with her great-grandfather earlier that day. She knew she wasn't supposed to speak with anyone about what had happened, but she was troubled at her decision.

In case anyone could overhear them, Madam Aveling hushed her granddaughter and led her into the office.

"I know everything," she told Aveling, "but not the finer details. And I don't need to know them. So, why are you having second thoughts?"

"Oh, Grandma," she sobbed. "Just the thought of being responsible for someone's death, I feel so guilty."

"Let's stop right there. First of all, did anyone tell you Harry was going to die? No." Madam Aveling's tone was cool. "I believe your great-grandfather has transported Harry back to his own country, where Harry will be locked up in a secure prison, where he belongs. I don't suppose it will have any modern facilities like the prisons in England, and he will not be getting any bail or parole, nor will he get a transfer to a mental hospital. The main thing is you don't need to worry about Harry, as you will not be seeing him ever again in this lifetime."

Madam Aveling put a comforting arm around her granddaughter. "Now calm down and remember that some things are best left unsaid."

Keen to change the subject, her grandmother asked if she had thanked the postman for his kindness.

"Not yet, Grandma," Aveling replied. "He did say before the police pulled us over that his wife would love to get my autograph."

Her grandmother laughed. "I think we can do a little better than that. How about you send him a gift of a new car?"

Aveling was stunned. "Grandma, I don't think I can afford to buy him a new car."

Madam Aveling was the one who looked surprised now. "I don't understand," she replied, frowning. "Have you spent all your money your grandfather left you?"

"What money, Grandma?"

"When your grandfather passed away, he left you ten million pounds in your savings account."

Aveling was totally confused. "I don't know anything about a savings account," she assured her grandmother. "The only money I have is the allowance my father puts into a bank account for me once a month."

"Sit there while I make a phone call," Madam Aveling instructed. And Aveling waited quietly while her grandmother talked to her bank manager.

Smiling now, Madam Aveling told her, "I didn't understand everything properly," she explained. "It seems your grandfather arranged with his solicitor and bank that you cannot use the account till you are twenty-one. I know it's now eighteen when you can legally be termed an adult, but sadly when your grandfather died you were still a little girl so he probably didn't think that through.

"Anyway, don't worry," she told the girl. "I've sorted it for now. I have just had the bank manager transfer one million pounds into your monthly account, so hopefully that should cover you till you reach twenty-one."

Aveling just sat like a statue, totally lost for words.

"Come on, young lady," her grandmother urged chirpily. "Time for tea."

*

The following morning, Madam Aveling asked Luke to take her granddaughter down to the village to get her out of the castle for a few hours and take her mind off things. But they returned very quickly, with Luke explaining they had been followed by newspaper reporters and photographers.

At dinner that evening, Prince Antony suggested that Luke could take Aveling to Paris to see the sites and enjoy some shopping.

Aveling was delighted with the idea and was quick to voice her agreement.

But when Prince Pip offered to take them there in his helicopter so they could see the whole of Paris, Prince Antony could not hide his annoyance.

Sensing his anger, Madam Aveling quickly jumped into the conversation. "Oh, what a good idea. We could all do with getting away for a break, so why don't we all go? There are so many places we haven't seen."

"Good thinking, my darling," said Prince Antony, looking relieved. "Why didn't I think of that?" And he smiled when he saw the look on his brother's face change from a grin to a frown.

CHAPTER 27: SURPRISE FAMILY

Prince Pip owned a villa in Perpignan in the south of France, so he invited then all to join him there after they had spent the weekend in Paris. He had asked for a raincheck on the Paris visit himself and would take his helicopter directly to his villa. That would give him time to sort out where everyone would be sleeping, and making sure Aveling's room was next to his.

He was still working on winning Aveling over, so he was making plans where he could spend time with her alone. But getting her away from his big brother wasn't going to be easy. And the bigger threat to him, as he saw it, was Luke,

So he had booked a trip for Luke to visit the nearby racing track on his own, with the chance to race some of the fastest cars ever made. He was confident Luke would not pass up such a treat, and that would free up Aveling to join Pip on his yacht. He knew his brother and Madam Aveling did not like taking trips on his yacht, as she suffered from seasickness, so he decided to wait until the last minute and offer Aveling a cruise around the harbour and get her alone. In the back of his mind, he was planning to get them both as far away from the villa as possible.

Knowing the area so well, it would be easy to find somewhere for the yacht to get into difficulty and have to stay at an out-of-the-way hotel overnight. In his head, he was sure he could wine and dine her then get her to sleep with him.

Pip was under the impression that if he showered her with treats, clothes, and jewellery, he could win her affection. Then, when the time was right, he was planning to propose. Confident of success, he already had the ring. It was white gold, with the biggest diamond any woman would die for, but he knew her grandmother would never agree to their marriage.

So for the time being, the first thing to do was to get rid of Luke, then all he needed was time to put all his plans into practice.

Once he heard from Prince Antony what time they were arriving at the villa, Prince Pip arranged the cars to collect them from the airport and booked the finest restaurant for dinner. As there had been so much publicity about the new princess being kidnapped in England, he decided it would be sensible to send two cars to the airport. He had also hired a new security team for the villa, with the guards being given orders that Aveling was not allowed to leave the villa without his say-so.

Unfortunately, though, the flight from Paris arrived early, and Prince Antony didn't want to hang around so just hired a car at the airport and they set off for the villa, with Luke driving.

Not long after they left the airport, he noticed that Aveling kept looking at the traffic behind them. "What's wrong?" he asked. "Why do you keep looking out the back window?"

"That dark blue car, I think it's following us," she replied. "I first saw it when we left the airport, and it is still behind us."

"It's probably a security team sent by Pip," Prince Antony assured her.

"I don't think so, Grandad. I can only just make out one driver."

Prince Antony immediately called his brother, who said it was not one of his security people. "I'll send my guys now," he told his older brother. "Tell Luke to take route nine onto the motorway, put the hazard lights on, and watch for two red vehicles. One will get in front of you and the other behind. Keep your speed down to fifty miles an hour and keep this phone line open while I get my guards moving."

After all she had been through, Aveling was growing more anxious and upset, but her grandmother assured there that it could not be Harry, and that she should let Prince Pip handle things. The motorway sign came up and Luke did as he was advised. And they hadn't been driving long when one red car pulled alongside them.

Another red car tried to manoeuvre behind them, but the blue car closed up the gap between them, shutting it out. When they relayed this information to Pip, he told them to hold tight. No sooner had he finished speaking than a French police car pulled up alongside them and flagged the blue car to pull over.

When they arrived at Pip's villa, Aveling was still stressed, so he offered to cancel the restaurant for dinner. Relieved to have arrived safely, she said they should still go. She'd been told about how spectacular the view was from the restaurant terrace overlooking the Mediterranean Sea.

After their luggage had been unpacked, Aveling and her grandmother changed for dinner and again she borrowed her grandmother's jewellery. The setting for their meal was stunning, and Aveling was thrilled to sit outside to eat and enjoy the amazing scenery.

As they chatted, Aveling asked Pip if he had heard anything from the police about that strange car that had followed them from the airport.

"They will let me know in the morning if there is a problem," he assured her.

Keen to quickly change the subject, Madam Aveling told everyone how her granddaughter had borrowed some of her jewellery again and that she wanted to help her choose some of her own.

The next morning, Aveling slept late, so when she finally got downstairs, she got her first proper look at Prince Pip's luxurious villa. She hadn't expected it to be so large, with huge marble columns, and modern furniture and décor – so different from her grandmother's castle.

When she finally found the kitchen, there were huge bifold doors leading into the garden. That morning they were fully open, and there was a strong and calming scent of lavender wafting its way in from the gardens.

When she finished her breakfast, Pip asked her if she would like to take a walk around the gardens. But as soon as she nodded, Luke jumped in and said he would like to go with them.

As they left the terrace, walking down two flights of steps, Pip was on one side of Aveling and Luke on the other. Luke had noticed the way the prince kept looking at Aveling, so knew he had his work cut out to stop her being taken in by the prince's prestige.

While he knew he couldn't match what Pip had to offer her, Luke still held the same feelings he had experienced the first day he met Aveling on the plane. He was convinced she was the girl for him.

The trio hadn't been walking long when Pip received a phone call. When he excused himself, saying he would meet them back on the patio later, Luke wondered if the call was from the French police. But he didn't want to make Aveling anxious again.

"I take it you like it here," he said. She was grinning from ear to ear and looked more relaxed than he had ever seen her.

"Well, who wouldn't?" she laughed. "It's just so out of this world."

"Aveling, you do know how I feel about you, don't you?"

She smiled. "Of course I do, or why else would you have joined us on our trip?"

"And you do know why Pip is doing all this for you?"

She frowned slightly. "Well, it's not just for me. This was a good time for all of us to get away from England and have a break."

Luke tried to choose his next words carefully. "You must realise that Pip has his own agenda, and if I am not mistaken, I think he is going to ask you to marry him."

Aveling shook her head. "Don't be so ridiculous, he's family! He's just being kind."

Frustrated at her naivety, Luke was unsure what to say. But she was standing so close to him that he could feel the hairs on the back of his neck stand up, and his heart was beating fast.

Slowly, as he didn't want to spook her after all she had been through, he drew her closer and hoped she wouldn't push him away. To his surprise, she leaned forward as if to give him permission. When his lips met hers for the first time, he felt his whole body responding and had to fight hard not to lose control.

Gently pulling away with a smile, he took her hand and they began to walk back to the villa. When they arrived, they were met by a stunning blonde woman, who looked as though she had just stepped out of the pages of a glossy magazine.

Prince Antony introduced the woman to Aveling and Luke as Pip's ex-wife, who was accompanied by her two children, Maria and Henry. The girl was about the same age as Aveling, and she could barely keep her eyes off Luke, while the boy was immediately drawn in by that invisible magnetism Aveling had with most men she met.

When Prince Pip emerged from the villa, the girl ran forward to hug him. "Papa, Papa, where have you been? I have missed you."

The boy studiously ignored him, while the ex-wife walked over to greet Pip with a kiss on both cheeks.

Although he looked a little taken aback to see his visitors, Pip swiftly recovered his composure and announced to everyone that the two young people were his ex-wife's children to her first husband.

Aveling was too busy chatting with Luke to notice that Pip seemed to be making a point that he had no biological children of his own. Sensing she was not paying attention, Pip realised he was going to have to work harder to gain her interest.

CHAPTER 28: THE BEST LAID PLANS

Unbeknown to Pip, his ex-wife had phoned ahead and asked the staff to prepare a surprise party for Henry's eighteenth birthday, and she had organised for a new sports car to be delivered and hidden inside the garage of the villa.

As the celebrations began, Pip tried to hide his surprise and stay calm. He wanted to press ahead with his plans to win over Aveling, so he wasn't happy at this change of arrangements.

Over lunch, Marie dropped another surprise on Pip. She announced that her mother was spending the next month in the United States, so she and her brother would be coming to stay with their stepfather.

It was soon clear that Maria was determined to commandeer Prince Pip's attention. She had changed the seating arrangements to ensure that she, not Aveling, was seated next to him. And she ordered the servants to move all Aveling's belongings into a room at the end of the hallway, as she always had the bedroom next to her stepfather.

For the rest of the day, and the following one, Aveling tried her best to get along with Maria but the girl ignored most of what she said. Things then became more stressful when she found out that the French had been in touch with the name of the driver of the blue car.

After spending so much time getting Harry out of her life, it seemed Aveling now had a stalker – Dr Valerie's son, Tommy.

Seeing that her granddaughter was a bag of nerves and clearly unsettled, Madam Aveling suggested that the best idea might be for her to return to England and spend some quiet time there with Luke. The suggestion did not sit well with the others, though.

Prince Antony said he needed to keep her close to protect her, and he was worried that the press would be all over the poor girl again. His brother knew that if Aveling returned to London with Luke, he would lose her. He was still hoping to get her alone on the yacht, but as soon as he mentioned a trip, both Henry and Maria announced that they wanted to come along.

Luke finally came up with an alternative idea by suggesting he took Aveling to spend some time with his parents who were working in China. As Aveling knew the language, and his parents worked up in the mountains in the panda clinic, her grandmother agreed this sounded like the best option. Prince Antony agreed, but then Maria threw a spanner in the works.

She demanded that she should be allowed to go along, as she had always wanted to see the pandas. But Prince Pip had experienced problems with business deals in China in the past, so he would not hear of it, insisting she would not be safe.

In the end, Prince Antony intervened and instructed that Luke should take Aveling to China for no more than four weeks, then he was to return her to the castle. And when Aveling indicated that she would like to go, he said he would organise flight tickets as soon as possible.

*

The following morning, Luke and Aveling took a flight to Paris then another flight to China, with strict instructions to return to England in four weeks.

Relieved to get the girl away from Prince Pip, Madam Aveling and her husband decided they would return to the castle. Pip's lifestyle and his stepchildren were driving Madam Aveling crazy. The siblings didn't know how to behave, and Maria was one of the most spoiled girls she had ever had to endure.

*

Once they were back at the castle, Prince Antony immersed himself in estate business while Madam Aveling caught up on paperwork. The only other person living at the castle was Lee.

Lee enquired whether Aveling had stayed on with Prince Pip in France and when she would be home. But when he learned of the plans and that she had gone to China to escape Tommy, he was furious.

He knew he had no right to control Aveling's life, but he was worried about Tommy turning up at the castle again. After questioning, the young man had been released by the French police, as they had no crimes to charge him with.

Determined to step up security, Lee organised installation of new cameras while Madam Aveling had all the windows fitted with new locks. As most of the windows were unreachable from outside, Prince Antony thought the new locks were a little over the top, but he was happy to go along with her to give her peace of mind.

While Madam Aveling kept herself busy, there was no doubt that she was missing her granddaughter and couldn't wait for her to come home. Even when Aveling had been painting in the conservatory, her grandmother had known she would see her for dinner, and she looked forward to their chats. But now the castle was so quiet.

One of James's duties was to regularly walk around the castle, checking all the rooms for broken windows, dampness, and even mouse droppings. On one occasion he found that a bird had fallen down an unused chimney and made a mess, with black soot everywhere.

Before Aveling returned, he was doing all the room checks when he ended up in storeroom where he would place all the items the old duke had no further use for. Madam Aveling had called it his dumping ground, but she could not bear to throw away any of the duke's things, even after she had remarried. On her orders, the room and its contents were left well alone.

That day, as James looked around, a mouse dashed from the fireplace and ran behind an old wooden crate. When James tried to move the crate, which was sealed with a metal band bearing Aveling's late Chinese grandfather's name, he found it was just too heavy.

Intrigued, he decided to go and get some help, but on his way downstairs he bumped into Madam Aveling. When he told her about the crate, she looked surprised. She had no recollection of it arriving and no idea what was inside. She suggested he left it till after dinner, when Lee would be back from working in the fields and could give him a hand.

A few hours later, Lee called James to report that he had spotted a strange campervan parked just outside the castle grounds, but when he tried to approach it, the van drove off. About an hour later it had returned again. Lee said he hadn't seen the driver, but after all that had happened he knew Madam would not take any chances.

When James went to the office and filled Madam Aveling and Prince Antony in on what Lee had seen, the prince immediately instructed him to get the Jeep, while he would follow in his car.

"When you get there, James, pull in front of the campervan, and I will pull in behind," the prince instructed.

Madam Aveling decided she wasn't being left out. "If it is Tommy, I need to have a little chat with that boy," she told them.

As James pulled out of the main gate, the campervan driver must have seen him and quickly pulled away before they could block him in. The prince wanted to give chase, but Madam Aveling stopped him, instructing James to follow the van and get the registration number, then meet them back at the castle.

It was almost thirty minutes later when James finally returned and explained that it had taken him some time to catch up with the van to get a note of the licence plate.

"Do you want me to call the police now?" Prince Antony asked her.

She shook her head. "Not yet. If we alert the police, things could be taken out of our hands. And anyway, what would they charge him with, parking outside of the grounds on a public road?"

"What do we do now then?" he asked.

"I want to take a little trip to see an old friend," she said with a sardonic grin. "I'd like you to find a current address for Dr Valerie, please. But," she warned, "don't use any phone lines or internet searches that can leave an electronic footprint."

She knew her husband had his own way of getting what he wanted, so she left him in the office and went through to arrange dinner. Just then Lee joined her from the fields, so she asked him if he had seen anything else suspicious.

"I did manage to get the number plate," he told her, and he handed over a slip of paper.

"James managed to get it this afternoon, but thanks anyway." But as she was speaking, she glanced at the piece of paper and didn't recognise the number Lee had written.

Suspicious now, she asked James to fetch the prince from her office with the registration number they had got earlier. When he did, they saw the numbers were different.

Madam Aveling realised that she had automatically jumped to the conclusion that Tommy was involved, but it was possible that the press were still hanging around since Aveling's kidnapping.

After a few minutes to think, she told Lee to go to the end of the field, staying covered in the treeline, and go as close to the van as possible without spooking the driver.

Later that evening he did as she had instructed, and while Madam Aveling and Prince Antony waited for his return, James asked what they had in mind.

"It all depends on what Lee says when he gets back," she told him. "If it is the press, we will need to call the police and leave it up to them. But as I said before, it's a public road so there is not much the police can do." She paused and sighed. "If it is Tommy, although he hasn't hurt Aveling, the last thing the girl needs now is to return from China to find someone stalking her."

A few minutes later Lee returned. "You won't believe this," he told them. "It's the same van, with one number plate on the back and a different number on the front."

"Well, that's a surprise!" replied Prince Antony. "Did you get a look at the driver?"

Lee shook his head. "No, he had the curtains closed. I think he must have been sleeping, but it was hard to get too close to the van."

"If it was the press, they would not have two different numbers on one van," Madam Aveling said. "It has to be Tommy, but I want to be sure before I take any action."

CHAPTER 29: CAMOUFLAGE

As Aveling and Luke were due to return from China at the end of the following week, Madam Aveling knew she had to act quickly. After throwing around a few ideas, they agreed that Lee would get up early and get as close to the campervan as possible, as they needed to identify the driver.

Lee had taken time to come to terms with his feelings for Aveling. And in the past few weeks while she had been away, he had realised that while he was extremely fond of her, he thought of her more as a sister than a girlfriend. But as he made his way across the field at the crack of dawn, he was determined to get all the information they needed to keep her safe.

While they were waiting for Lee's return, James suggested he could call the hospital to ask for an appointment to see Doctor Tommy. "It would give us some idea of his whereabouts. If he was at work, he couldn't be parked outside the gates."

Before they could do so, Lee arrived.

"It's definitely Tommy," he said, breathless from hurrying back. "I saw him getting out of the van to pee."

Madam Aveling frowned. "Well, at least we know now. So, I will be taking that little trip after all. Antony," she asked her husband, "did you manage to get those details I need?"

"Of course, my darling, it's all taken care of," he assured her. "I will be coming with you, but who else should we take?"

"On this occasion, I think just Lee to do the driving," she replied.

It was still early as they set off, but they knew they had a long drive ahead of them.

When they reached their destination and slowed down outside a large Victorian terraced house, Lee said he saw the curtains move at one of the windows, so he was fairly sure that someone was at home. Not wanting the car to be recognised, Madam Aveling told him to stop a little further down the road and asked him and Prince Antony to wait in the car.

As she walked up the driveway, the front door opened, and for the first time in years Madam Aveling and Dr Valerie found themselves face-to-face again. Surprisingly, the doctor reached out to take her hands then pulled her into a hug as though they were long lost sisters.

Being led through to the kitchen, Madam Aveling was keen that this should not be seen as a social visit. She didn't want to hurt Dr Valerie in any way, but she might have to take action against Tommy.

Valerie offered tea as they sat down at the table for a moment, just staring at each other.

Dr Valerie spoke first. "I know why you are here. There is only one reason I can think of... it's Tommy, isn't it?"

"Yes," Madam Aveling confirmed. "I hope you realise I would never have come if I didn't respect what you tried to do for me. But I cannot sit idly by when I feel my granddaughter might get hurt."

"No, no," Dr Valerie replied. "He would never hurt the girl. It all started when he heard she had been shot in China. He has been beside himself with worry, and all he ever wanted to do was protect her."

"Well, it's time for him to come home and leave my granddaughter's safety to me." Madam Aveling's tone was cool. "As you know, she is my only grandchild and things are never easy when you have a title. If you have been watching the press, you will know that the same man kidnapped her again, so I cannot allow any man to get that close to her. She now has her own bodyguards, so you need to call Tommy off."

"I have tried to phone him every day, but he just won't listen to me," the doctor admitted.

Madam Aveling shrugged. "Valerie, you know me better than most people, so you are aware of what I can do." She paused briefly when she saw Dr Valerie becoming emotional. "There is something else I should like to ask you. Why on earth did you write that damned book, *Damaged Mind*? I heard it's now on the bestselling list, and I am perfectly aware how much money you have made from my nightmare of a life."

Dr Valerie did not reply and the kitchen fell silent again as the two women sat looking at each other.

"I know you are as fond of your grandson as I am of my granddaughter, but I cannot sit by and allow this to continue any longer." Madam Aveling's tone was icy. "So I will ask you just once again, can you call him off? If he cares about the girl, he will leave her alone. He can leave me his phone number, and I will pass it on if she ever asks for it or needs his help in the future. But he has got just twenty-four hours to leave… or I will act." Then she stood up to leave.

CHAPTER 30: AVELING'S RETURN

It was a cold damp day when James came into the office to tell Madam Aveling and the prince he had just received a phone call from Luke to say they had landed safely at the airport. They wouldn't be back at the castle, however, for a few more days. Luke's parents had invited them back to their English home for a few days, as they had all got on so well in China, and Luke was keen to show her around the village where he had grown up.

Madam Aveling was delighted to hear they had arrived back in the UK safely, but as Tommy had not moved his campervan since her visit to Doctor Valerie, she knew it was time to get rid of him.

Keen not to hurt Doctor Valerie with her actions, Madam Aveling decided to try a different approach, and she wrote Tommy a letter.

Dear Tommy,

I just wanted to say thank you for all your kind help for my granddaughter Aveling, and for getting in touch with me at a time when she needed me the most.

I know how you much you care for her, but I need you to leave and take a step back to let the girl find her own way. I will ask her if she is willing to write to you in person, if that is alright with you. I have your address and phone number from your grandmother.

I know if Aveling hears you have been parking outside the castle, she could feel very anxious. So please step back and allow her to grow and make up her own mind.

Thank you,

Madam Aveling

Madam Aveling had given the matter a lot of thought and hoped the gentle approach was the best. But if it didn't work, she would need to ask her father-in-law to come for a visit and take Tommy back with him to join Harry.

She didn't really want to take that step, but she had already tried talking to his grandmother, so if the letter didn't work she had no choice.

Late that night, Lee took the letter and placed it gently under the windscreen wipers of the campervan.

The next morning, the campervan had gone when Lee went to check. And over the next few days there was no further sight of the vehicle outside the gates.

*

On the day Aveling was due to return, all the staff were busy preparing her room, putting fresh flowers throughout the castle, and lighting the fires to make all the rooms warm and cosy.

As the car pulled up into the courtyard, everyone was there to welcome her, and Aveling stepped out of the car with a huge smile.

Over dinner that evening, it seemed impossible to stop the girl from talking. She regaled them with her visit to the panda bear clinic for the first time, and by the time she had finished talking, everyone had been well educated about the animals.

Madam Aveling had never seen the girl so excited. Even when dinner had finished, Aveling kept the stories coming, and she admitted that she wanted to return to China as soon as possible. When Luke finally managed to get a word in, he explained that his parents were hoping to go back there next season and had said that Aveling was more than welcome to go with them.

It was very late when they all retired that night. Aveling and her grandmother were already in bed, but Luke took a few minutes to talk quietly to Prince Antony downstairs.

"Lee told me all about Tommy," he explained, "so I can't help worrying about Aveling."

"There's no need for that, Luke. We have had security cameras fitted to all the hallways and landing, and more in the kitchen. In fact, I was joking that we had fitted more cameras than I can count." Prince Antony laughed, then his face became serious when he added, "Aveling is well covered in here, but I am a little concerned about outside."

"I don't remember seeing any vans parked outside, but I did see a few cars as we pulled up the driveway," Luke replied. "We both thought it might be the press just looking to get the first photos of us returning home. But if you think Tommy is going to return, what should I tell Aveling?"

"For now, don't say anything. Let me take care of things, and you get off to bed."

*

The following morning, Lee was up at the crack of dawn to make sure Tommy had not returned. On his way back to report to Madam Aveling, he spotted a group of men hiding just on the outskirts of the forest. He wasn't sure but thought one of them did look a lot like Tommy, while the other two seemed to have cameras hanging around their necks. But when he approached them, they dispersed in different directions.

Castle Keys had never been open to the public, but over the years it had moved with the times and opened its grounds to paying customers. Although there were very few farm animals, the castle boasted a first-class salmon farm, award-winning horse stables, and one of the best shooting sites for game, pheasant, and other birds.

After Lee gave his report about the three individuals he had seen, Madam Aveling experienced a real sense of disappointment. If Tommy was still there, she would have some very difficult decisions to make.

First, she asked the prince to pick two of the security guards who were currently out working on the estate. The men were told to put on their camouflage uniforms, ensure they were always in radio contact, and to stay close to the castle so that no unauthorised person was allowed to enter.

The prince and Lee then drove over to the old barn, which looked rundown and barely used from the outside, but inside the old duke had turned it into a well-fitted out barracks with an assortment of firepower and everything ex-military men would need. He had always told Madam Aveling to keep the men well fed and with a roof over their heads, as he himself had once lived on the streets as a young man after the war.

Over the years men came and went, but there were currently six, all ex-military, living in the barracks. Another six men, who worked on the land, mostly lived around the village, but they would all gather for lunch at the barn.

It was lunchtime when the prince arrived there, so he took the opportunity to address everyone. He asked them to uniform up and then explained who and what they would be looking for. He instructed them to go out in groups of three to patrol the grounds.

"If you come across anybody who is not a castle worker, take them to the old gatehouse, and if they refuse, put them in cuffs. We can hold them there until later in the day when Lee will call the police to have them arrested for trespass."

By the end of that first day, they had rounded up more than expected and were holding eight men and two women, but there was no sign of Tommy. So the next day they were instructed to continue with their patrols.

Luke had been filled in on everything that was happening and asked to stay close to Aveling, but not to tell her anything about what was happening outside. They all knew it would be difficult to prevent her finding out, as the staff inside the castle were aware there was something going on and rumours were everywhere.

One of the young cleaners was working quietly in the conservatory while Aveling was painting, when suddenly she saw a face at the window. Already anxious about what was going on outside, the girl let out a loud scream.

Luke had been sitting at the side of the conservatory reading and had just left the room to get some drinks when the cleaner screamed. He rushed immediately back to see what was happening.

While the girl explained what she had seen, Luke could see Aveling was going into panic mode. She was breathing heavily, gulping in air, and her face was chalk white. Luke put his arms gently around her to reassure her everything was ok and explained that the man the maid had seen was just one of the workers on security detail.

As the girl, still shaking, was led back to the kitchen to calm down, Aveling was trying hard to keep her feelings to herself. She was just so worried that if she made a fuss, things would only get worse.

CHAPTER 31: THE FIND

Everyone was still very jumpy, and Madam Aveling was trying to think of something to keep her granddaughter's mind busy.

After breakfast Aveling announced that she would like to take Luke down to the stables to show him around. She was hoping to teach him how to ride, but she was still a novice herself.

"Perhaps the stable manager could help us," she suggested.

Prince Antony thought it was a splendid idea but offered to be the one to teach them.

Before he could finish, Madam Aveling quickly interrupted. "No way. I don't want you back on a horse, not after your last fall."

"Oh, darling," he replied, "everybody takes falls when riding, so don't worry." But seeing the look on her face, he quickly invited her to join them and promised he would not mount up. "It will keep us all busy and our minds off everything," he added.

At the stables, the manager found the two gentlest horses and led them both to the compound which was encircled by fencing. With his help, Luke and Aveling managed to mount up.

"I didn't realise we would be so high off the ground," Luke called out anxiously, as the horses were led slowly around the arena.

They trotted around for some time, the stable manager maintaining his hold on the strap keeping Luke's horse completely under his control. But Aveling was eager to go out over the estate, adding that she knew how to ride.

The manager looked over at the way she was holding her reins and shook his head. "I don't think that would be a good idea," he said.

Before she could grumble to her grandmother, he went on, "I don't know who taught you how to ride, but you are holding the reins all wrong. If the horse takes off too fast, you could get hurt."

Agreeing, the prince asked, "Who allowed you to ride like that?"

"It was Mary, on the Glenhall Estate," Aveling replied.

"Well, that explains it." Madam Aveling glanced at her watch. "Time for lunch, so let's all call it a day. Next time, after you get some more lessons, I will allow you both to take a trot around the track that is used for training."

Aveling was a little disappointed at first, but she had to smile when Luke commented that he wasn't too sure if riding was for him. On the way back to the castle, he admitted he had never been so scared in his whole life and was more than happy to be back on the ground.

After lunch they were joined by Lee, who had popped in to brief Madam Aveling on the trespassers. He informed her that they had picked up another few, but there were no major problems, and still no Tommy.

"You said the other day that you wanted me to help James with an old wooden crate," he said. "I could do it now, if you like?"

While he headed off to find James, Aveling and Luke made their way to the conservatory. The girl was keen to get back to her painting, and Luke was happy to sit near her and read. Prince Antony had given him a copy of the book Doctor Valerie had penned, *Damaged Mind*, telling him that it could possibly inform him better than any gossip.

After half an hour, Luke had already reached chapter five and was finding it difficult to stop. So when Aveling asked him to pass her some tissues, he didn't answer as his concentration was on the book.

Intrigued, Aveling went over to see what he was reading, but the movement alerted Luke and he quickly closed the book before she could reach him. When she asked why, he told her the book was too dark, and he didn't want her to be upset by the contents.

Aveling wasn't convinced. She quickly snatched it from his hands then opened the book halfway through. After reading a few sentences, she closed it with a thud. "How dare you read a book like that?" she stormed. "It's disgusting."

"Aveling, I am so sorry. I didn't know it was going to be like that," he apologised.

"Where did you get it from? I don't believe Grandma would have such a book in our home."

His face drained of all colour, Luke explained that the prince had asked him to read it because it was all about her grandmother. "He thought it would help me understand why things have to be kept guarded."

Aveling took a breath then sat down beside him. "In that case," she said, "I want to read it, too. We can do it together, chapter by chapter."

Luke, still uneasy, said he would only agree if she told no-one that he had shown her the book.

*

Madam and her husband were in the office when they were joined by James and Lee, carrying the wooden crate. Lee had brought wire cutters and they all gathered around for a closer look. When she studied the seal, Madam Aveling suddenly remembered that the crate had arrived just a few weeks after the duke had passed away, and she had been so busy with arrangements for the funeral and the estate that she had told the staff to put it in the storeroom then forgotten all about it.

Lee was just about to cut the seal to remove the wire when she stopped him. "Wait," she said. "This is from Avelin's Chinese grandfather, so she should be here to see this."

James went quickly to the conservatory and returned with Aveling and Luke. With bated breath and a sense of excitement, they all gathered around the crate while the wire was cut. When the crate lid was prized off, a bronze sphere stood before them.

As Aveling moved forward to touch it gently, Luke asked, "What is it?"

The sphere was covered in what appeared to be Chinese markings, but even with her knowledge of the language, Aveling could not make any sense of it.

Using the trolley jack, due to the item's weight, Lee manoeuvred it to sit at one side of the fireplace. They could all then see that it was a very attractive piece of bronze carving, the size of a large, inflated beach ball, so the prince decided it would be a shame to return it to the old room to collect dust.

After they'd all studied the bronze for several minutes and were still unable to guess its use, Luke and Aveling decided to go to her grandmother's library to dig through the late duke's books. Maybe they could find more information there.

CHAPTER 32: JADE

Everything was settling down at the castle. The security staff were still on high alert, but there had only been a few members of the press hanging around outside at times, trying to get photos of the new princess.

Madam Aveling regarded the press pack as a nuisance but accepted that sadly this would become a normal part of Aveling's life now. Thankfully, there had been no more sightings of Tommy.

As Madam Aveling was still disappointed that her granddaughter's eighteenth birthday party had been interrupted by the arrival of the police, she decided to organise a St Valentine's ball to cheer everyone up. But this time she was going all out. The room was decorated with moons, stars, and hearts, while invitations had been sent out to over one hundred guests, and the party would end with fireworks using the castle turrets as a backdrop.

*

On the night of the ball, there were over twenty contract workers engaged to do all the serving, and as the guests arrived Madam Aveling thought she had never seen her granddaughter look so happy. Luke was her constant companion, having been asked by the prince to stay close to Aveling in case of any trouble.

As the night progressed, things were going smoothly, but Madam Aveling had a feeling something wasn't right. She voiced her concerns to her husband, who reassured her that the security men were on alert, covering all the entrances and exits, and there was someone in the kitchen disguised as a chef.

Madam Aveling was never comfortable in crowds of people, so she retired to her office for a while for some peace and where she could still hear the music from the party. She was looking forward to watching the fireworks light up the sky and decided that the best view would be from Aveling's bedroom.

Prince Antony had promised to meet her there, but the bedroom was empty when she arrived. After a few minutes, though, she felt as though she was not alone, and as she looked around the room, she saw Aveling's belongings scattered all over the floor.

That was the last thing she remembered until she came round, lying on the carpet, with her husband anxiously calling her name.

"What the hell happened?" she groaned.

"When I arrived, someone pushed past me and ran out of the room. I didn't get a look at the face, but it was definitely a woman. She was wearing a silver evening gown with a black shoe. Then I saw you lying on the floor…" he explained, his voice tailing off with emotion.

"Is Aveling safe?" she asked.

"The castle has been put into lockdown," he assured her. "The guests have been enjoying the fireworks from the courtyard, so they wouldn't hear the noise of the chains when the drawbridge was lifted. The only way out is to swim in freezing water."

The prince carried his wife to their bedroom, placing her gently on the bed where he checked her over. He couldn't find any wounds, so suggested she had possibly fainted with shock, but he wanted her to stay in bed till they caught the thief.

The firework display was coming to an end, so he left her to rest, posting a guard just outside her door. The thought of someone loose in the castle worried him.

He knew people would want to leave soon, but every single person would have to be searched first. When everyone returned to the ballroom, ready to say their farewells and collect their belongings, Prince Antony took the microphone and explained that there had been a situation and that everyone's invitation card would have to be checked and matched before they could leave.

A few guests began to grumble, becoming more unhappy as the clock ticked into the early hours. As they left one by one, their mobile phones were confiscated to be examined later, in the hope of spotting the thief on any photos or videos.

Finally, when there were only about twenty guests left to be checked, a woman suddenly grabbed one of the remaining guests, pushing her hard, then trying to escape.

Immediately recognising her, Lee lunged at the woman and dragged her to feet and let rip with words Aveling had never heard before,

The prince looked confused, as the women was not wearing a silver gown. But Aveling, immediately realising who it was, lifted the hem of the dress to show that it was silver on the inside, then grabbed the woman's evening bag and emptied it onto the floor. As everyone looked on, the three pieces of jade fell to the floor.

"Why, Mary? Why?" Aveling screamed at her.

"What the hell is going on?" Luke demanded.

To his amazement, Aveling explained that the woman was Mary Glenhall – someone he had heard a lot about but never met – and she had clearly got past security and unnoticed by wearing a wig and glasses.

CHAPTER 33: AFTER THE BALL

"Why did you want to steal my jade? It's no good to you," Aveling snapped.

"No, but I know how important it is to you," Mary spat back. "That stupid bit of silk, and those three broken pieces of jade."

As Aveling picked her jade up from the floor, Mary was accusing her of destroying her relationship with first Harry, then Lee. Shouting at the top of her voice, Mary was completely out of control and lunged at Aveling. Luke pulled Aveling out of harm's way just in time to prevent her from getting hurt.

"She's not worth it," he told Aveling. "Lee has called the police, so they are on their way."

Luke had previously been told by the prince what Mary and her brother had arranged for Aveling, and how it was Mary's boyfriend Harry who had caused the girl so much pain. He could see how upset Aveling was at coming face-to-face with Mary again, and he was eager to get her away as quickly as possible.

As the police arrived and handcuffed Mary to lead her away, Luke took Aveling's hand and they headed upstairs. Their bedrooms were on the same floor, but when they reached his room first, Aveling leaned in for a kiss.

"Don't leave," he whispered. "I know it's late, but if I try to sleep I will just be tossing and turning, worrying about you. I can see how this evening has upset you."

Aveling put her arms around his neck and they slowly kissed again before he opened his bedroom door and slowly led her inside.

They walked together to the bed, where they both sat down, still embracing but not saying a word.

When Aveling lay back and pulled him down on top of her, they kissed again. Luke was beginning to lose control, but he knew he had to wait till she decided to make the next move.

When she reached up to open his shirt buttons, he could not hold on any longer and carefully unzipped her dress, then loosened her bra. As he did so, he gently lowered himself to kiss her breasts then continued lower and lower till he reached her knickers. He slowly eased them off to reveal her mound of black pubic hair, unable to resist kissing it.

Pulling his shirt and trousers off, he lay back down beside her and kissed her as she had never been kissed before. Then he entered her slowly, very slowly. For him it was beginning to feel like heaven but also torture, as he needed to come. He tried so hard to hold off, but then it was too late and he felt the rush of sperm leave his body.

The pair lay without speaking while he continued to kiss her, and when he began to stroke her inner thighs and she moaned quietly in delight, he soon got another erection. This time he wanted to keep things under control, but when she seemed to lift her pelvis up, for the first time in his life he felt a woman so close to orgasm. He could feel her muscles tightening around his penis, and he was again totally out of control. As she orgasmed, so did he.

When they were both spent, he raised his body off her and they slipped under the bedsheet and fell fast asleep.

When Luke woke the next morning, her naked body was still lying next to him, and he found it impossible not to touch her. After a few minutes she rolled over to look at him with her sleepy green eyes. Overcome with emotion, he kissed her as he gently opened her legs and entered her again.

Afterwards, Luke got up to use the toilet and returned to find Aveling asleep again. This time, he gently kissed her on the forehead so as not to wake her, then he dressed and went downstairs. It was still early and most of the staff were just starting work. As he was sitting at the dining table, Lee arrived and poured himself a coffee. Luke wasn't sure how, but it seemed as though Lee knew what had happened last night.

"Just remember," Lee said quietly, "if you ever hurt her, I will kill you." And with that he finished his coffee and left the room.

A few hours later, two uniformed police officers arrived to be met by Lee at the front door. They informed him that Mary had been released with a caution and that no further action would be taken. Lee was angry and had no idea how he was going to tell the rest of the family that Mary had not been charged.

Madam Aveling was still sleeping till late, but when she was told later, she wasn't surprised to hear Mary had walked away. Aveling just wanted the damn girl out of her life.

*

When the pieces of jade had been recovered the previous night at the end of the ball, Aveling had picked them up off the floor and left them on the hall table to take up to her room. But she had completely forgotten about them in all the drama.

Later the next day, deciding to destress herself by doing some painting, she went to the conservatory in the hope of enjoying a few hours alone. Barely an hour had passed when Luke joined her, but he never said a word and just sat down to continue reading his book.

Aveling was so engrossed with her painting of blue poppies that she was surprised when Luke gently tapped her on the shoulder to tell her it was time for tea.

Looking up at the clock, she was shocked to see the time. "Already?" she replied. "I don't feel like I have been painting for three hours. Okay, I will just clean out my brushes. Why don't you go ahead, and I will join you all shortly?"

When she met up with the rest of the family in the dining room, there seemed to be quite a commotion.

"What the hell is going on now?" she asked. "Why is everybody so excited?"

Holding out her three pieces of jade, Luke explained that James had been moving some mail off the hallway table and had picked up the jade to take the pieces upstairs. It was at that point he'd noticed that the patterns on each piece was different.

"It looks as though it was never intended to be a bangle, but a key," he told her.

"But a key to what?" she asked. "An item still in China?"

James replied, "No, Aveling. When I picked up your jade, I recognised the same pattern was on the brass globe I found in the old store room, and I am sure that's where we need to place the pieces."

Everyone stood up and made their way quickly to her grandmother's office, where the brass globe still stood beside the fireplace. James handed the three pieces of jade over to Aveling, and she slowly matched up the shapes on the globe with the jade.

When she pushed the first piece into the globe, they all heard a definite click, and again with the second piece. Everyone watched excitedly as she fitted the last piece and they heard the final click, not knowing what to expect.

Suddenly the globe began to open like a giant lotus flower. And as the final petals opened, there was a huge diamond, set in gold, sitting inside.

"Oh, my goodness," Aveling breathed. "Grandma, I don't understand. How did it get here, and why didn't anyone open the crate before?"

There was no reply and only a strange pause in the conversation, as Madam Aveling then spotted a piece of paper in the shape of a water lily. As she opened the paper, it was covered in Chinese symbols but she could not read them.

They all looked towards Aveling, who was still cradling the diamond in her hands. Her grandmother handed her the paper and Aveling began to read what turned out to be a letter.

> *"This stone was given to the lady concubine who was known as the lady Gemini, as a wedding gift from the Emperor," she read.*
>
> *"If you are now reading this note, you are the new owner of the stone. When the late Emperor presented her with the stone, on the reverse of the gold surrounding the diamond it was carved with the words: To the brightest star in all the sky, my darling little Gemini."*

Aveling turned to her grandmother and reminded her that these were the same words as on the back of the pendant she had been given her to wear in London.

"How is that possible, Grandma?" she asked.

Madam could only guess that her late husband must have left it as a clue, but more than that she just didn't know.

> *Aveling read on, "It is believed the Emperor had the diamond set into a gold and jade mount to be incorporated into the new concubine's palace pass, to be worn around Gemini's waist.*

As they had all been condemned to die that day, one of the other concubines who was also being taken to the hanging room told little Gemini that if she had anything of any value she needed to conceal it in her clothing. So when little Gemini escaped the hanging silks that day, she still had the diamond pass around her waist. She didn't understand why they were being taken away, but when one of the other concubines began to cry, little Gemini guessed it wasn't good.

"*It was only when her blood brother told her what to do in the room they were now all being forced to enter, and Gemini saw all the silk hanging from the roof, that she began to understand. Her legs almost gave way, while some of the other girls began to sob or struggle. Without her brother's instruction, she would have died that day. As she watched the other concubines, her heart began to feel heavy, and her eyes began to fill with tears, as she too had the silk hung around her neck.*

"*Her brother whispered, 'Don't cry, and don't forget what I told you.' Then he pushed something into her mouth.*

"*As she watched the girls die one by one, she wasn't too sure if her brother would manage to save her, but she would do all she could to stay alive. She eventually passed out.*"

Aveling passed the stone around the others to let them have a closer look, then she quietly replaced the letter in the same place it had been taken from. When everyone had finished examining the stone, she replaced it in the globe and removed the three pieces of jade. As she did so, the globe began to slowly close again.

Madam Aveling suggested they needed to find a safe place to keep the globe and asked Aveling if that was alright with her.

"Yes, of course. But, Grandma, don't you find it strange that the duke gave you the name of Gemini all those years ago, when the concubine was also called Gemini?"

"Yes, I do," her grandmother agreed, "but I guess that's just fate. Do you have any more questions?"

Aveling looked closely at her grandmother, frowning, thinking that was a strange reply. After a few minutes, she said, "I only have one more question. Doctor Valerie finished her book by saying that you said your name was not Aveling."

There was a brief pause.

"So, Grandma, what is your real name?"

www.ingramcontent.com/pod-product-compliance
Lightning Source LLC
LaVergne TN
LVHW091251080426
835510LV00007B/220